'This book goes to the heart of the eternal and under-reported suffering of the Rohingya. Forced out of what once was Burma and now is Myanmar, most are in exile in Bangladesh and beyond. An important story of our times.'

— Jon Snow

'This book paints a deep, complicated and appalling picture: of one million people who have fled danger but now face immense risks from those they thought would protect them. While documenting the harm done by the UN and the Bangladeshi state, Ahmed humanises those normally dehumanised—the refugees.'

— Aditya Chakrabortty, *The Guardian*

'A haunting and poetic, yet incisive and grounded, account of the tragedies that have befallen the Rohingya, of the realities of a people living almost entirely in exile, and of their struggles to maintain dignity and hope in the face of persecution and betrayal.'

— Kenan Malik, author, broadcaster and *Observer* columnist

'*I Feel No Peace* is a tender, forensic, harrowing and beautifully human portrait of the Rohingya, a people persecuted beyond measure. Ahmed has produced an exceptional work of journalism which promises to inspire change for the better.'

— Musa Okwonga, author, podcaster and musician

'This is a remarkable and vivid testament to the results of Myanmar's genocide of the Rohingya. A striking portrait of a people forced on the run—in all their suffering, bravery and determination. A must-read.'

— Azeem Ibrahim, author of *The Rohingyas*
and *Authoritarian Century*

'A strikingly urgent and necessary book, giving voice to the world's most silenced people. A fierce roar of resistance against the greed, racism and violence that have been largely ignored by the global community. This is a book to be read by all.'

— Zana Fraillon, author of *The Bone Sparrow*

'Kaamil Ahmed is both a journalist and friend to many Rohingya. This is what makes his book come alive. With great detail, he tells the story of Myanmar's genocidal attacks, the diverse journeys of many refugees, as well the resilience of the Rohingya people.'

— John Quinley, Senior Human Rights Specialist, Fortify Rights

'Kaamil Ahmed's book fills a glaring void in the literature on one of the world's worst examples of cruelty and dispossession. It promises to bring much-needed attention to the catastrophe of the Rohingya and deserves to be widely read.'

— Christopher Lamb, President, Australia Myanmar Institute

'Readers wanting to learn about Rohingya refugees and understand the complexity of their current plight will not be disappointed by Ahmed's book, which provides both personal accounts of the Rohingya's unfathomable hardships and historical events that contextualise the protracted crisis.'

— Mary Shepard Wong, Professor in the Department of Sociology, Azusa Pacific University, and editor of *Teaching for Peace and Social Justice in Myanmar*

I FEEL NO PEACE

KAAMIL AHMED

I Feel No Peace

Rohingya Fleeing Over Seas and Rivers

HURST & COMPANY, LONDON

First published in the United Kingdom in 2023 by
C. Hurst & Co. (Publishers) Ltd.,
New Wing, Somerset House, Strand, London, WC2R 1LA
© Kaamil Ahmed, 2023
All rights reserved.

Distributed in the United States, Canada and Latin America by
Oxford University Press, 198 Madison Avenue, New York, NY 10016,
United States of America.

The right of Kaamil Ahmed to be identified as the author
of this publication is asserted by him in accordance with the
Copyright, Designs and Patents Act, 1988.

A Cataloguing-in-Publication data record for this book
is available from the British Library.

ISBN: 9781787389311

This book is printed using paper from registered, sustainable
and managed sources.

www.hurstpublishers.com

Printed in Great Britain by Bell and Bain Ltd, Glasgow

CONTENTS

AUTHOR'S NOTE

This is a book based around a single phrase: *Oshanti Lage*. It is a word I heard hundreds of times in conversations with Rohingya but never fully comprehended, so I tried to package it into an emotion English-speaking audiences would understand. When I asked the Rohingya I met over many years of reporting how they felt about the situations they were in, they said they felt *Oshanti*. I interpreted it with straightforward English words—sadness, anger, worry. The term was so ubiquitous I became frustrated with it as an answer and tried to prompt different responses by altering the ways I asked about their emotions. But it was so common because it was the perfect word for their condition. To understand it I had to look at its literal meaning, not its functional interpretations. *Oshanti* is the negation of *Shanti*: peace. "I feel no peace", they were telling me. Individually, it may have referred only to the scenarios they described, but perhaps there was a reason it resonated throughout the Rohingya nation. After all, it has been a long time since there has been any peace for them to feel.

I was shocked when I first encountered them as a people, through a TV screen, as an Al Jazeera reporter interviewed a Rohingya woman stepping off a boat from Myanmar. She spoke in words and cadences that were oddly familiar to the version of

Bengali I had heard growing up, yet also strange enough that I could not really understand her. I could not fathom who these people were, people I had never heard of, people who were being kicked out of Myanmar where the state called them Bengalis but who were turned back from Bangladeshi shores. Back in 2009, few people spoke of who they were, this Muslim minority from the most western frontiers of Myanmar. I was eager to learn about them, keen to make reporting on them a part of the career I had yet to embark on. By 2015, I achieved this when I first visited the decades-old refugee camps that housed hundreds of thousands of them in Bangladesh. It was then that I met Nobi, one of the people who I will return to repeatedly in this book. We met because Rohingya suffering had increased to the point the media were able to dub it a "crisis"—when thousands of Rohingya were stranded at sea after a transnational trafficking network, built through the smuggling of Rohingya to Southeast Asia, had been busted. While most journalists rushed to the Southeast Asian nations they were being turned away from, I went down to the Bangladeshi camps that many of them were leaving. I wanted to know why any Rohingya no longer in Myanmar would risk such a dangerous journey.

This was when I first began to discover that there was no peace for the Rohingya, wherever they went. Nobi had lived his whole life in Nayapara, a refugee camp established in Bangladesh in the early 1990s but which few people knew about, where he had always been told he could not work, study, or even move beyond its boundaries. His family had fled Myanmar for their safety, but his generation was stranded in a state of statelessness and exploited wherever they sought escape. A whole trafficking industry had been built off the Rohingya desire for more free-dom (which they had heard could be found in Malaysia) and profited from their desperation by extorting ransoms from their families. Those who stayed behind could be kidnapped; arrested;

pressured into muling drugs for local kingpins; or, if they were vulnerable women, forced into prostitution. Some sought alternative options in Saudi Arabia or India and found life no less uncertain. They had no papers and so they were invisible, forever at risk of ending up in prison. You could almost map it out: whichever route they took in search of something better, there was a system that exploited them for profit. The story of Rohingya persecution in Myanmar—of military operations in 1978 and 1991, of their citizenship being stripped, of pogroms in 2012—had been reported to an extent, but the full scale of their *Oshanti* was not confined to those borders.

But eyes glazed over whenever I spoke of them, and continued to do so until 2017 when suddenly they became newsworthy. Myanmar launched its largest ever military operation against the Rohingya, forcing 700,000 into Bangladesh and making the camps Nobi had grown up in the world's largest. There were now more Rohingya in Bangladesh than in Myanmar itself. So, I returned, and saw everything had changed. The camps were now unrecognisable in their size and filled with trauma fresher than ever. My guide through all of this was Yassin—like Nobi, another young educator who had freshly arrived in Bangladesh and was eager to tell his people's story. He had no journalistic training but had an open ear and was aware of every story in the camp. He rarely appears in this book but he was a crucial part of it all, by my side for so much of the journey.

I also saw that the experiences of Nobi's generation, who knew nothing but the life of refugees, were not being listened to. In fact, the world's aid workers, who rushed in and stayed in luxury hotels, called this a "new crisis". Many were completely unaware that there had been Rohingya in these camps for thirty years, that their organisations, especially the UN, had worked with them—and sometimes even against them. This book is about the Rohingya pursuit of peace beyond Myanmar. It is about those who sought it many decades ago and those who seek it now, in the aftermath of Myanmar's 2017 military operations. And it is about the international machine they pass through, which claims to offer peace but has failed to protect them.

PART 1

1

TULA TOLI

August 2017

In the absence of peace, the inhabitants of Tula Toli learned to live with quiet. The Rohingya who belonged to this village knew they could not move, not unless they were to run, and so they practised stillness. They lived with what was around them; fishing the rivers that formed the nervous system of a Rohingya heartland, farming the land of their forefathers and raising livestock. They gave birth at home and sought medical advice from local healers because hospitals lay beyond impossible barriers. They educated themselves by exchanging the knowledge they had among them. Their aspirant youth abandoned hopes of studying at university. Mosques sat locked, loudspeakers muted, as hidden congregations instead prayed in whispers inside homes. In the forests that shielded the village from view, they foraged the raw materials to make goods they could not buy, harvested trees for fuel and found the bamboo they wove into roofs for their homes. They sat out storms in silence and, when the worst of them came, sought shelter in the shadow of the nearby Mayu

3

mountains, the green giants that watch over the Rohingya heartland in Myanmar's northern Rakhine State. They had run several times before from the military, the Tatmadaw, only to be returned to Myanmar, told by their hosts and the United Nations that it was now safe—there was peace.

Their returns had taught them otherwise. They found they were still killed by a military that bore down on them, a state that rejected them and a public that had learned to hate them and whose mobs joined the soldiers. Relationships with their neighbours decayed until there were no longer links between communities. Tula Toli learned over several decades to live not only outside the state but also within the limits it set. They directed their gaze to the ground to avoid locking eyes with the military. They did not call this peace, but they hoped it would stay the genocide.

At 30 years old, Momtaz Begum had only ever known this uncomfortable quiet. She had never felt peace. By the time she was born, her people had already become accustomed to the Rohingya's muted version of life and, when she married, Momtaz and her husband started teaching their five children to live in the same way. Their days blended into a series of typical village tasks: her husband farmed and she ensured the family's lives ticked over, collecting fuel from the forests, drawing water from the ground and watching over their children. Her parents lived in another home and her sisters, who were all married, lived with their husbands in different corners of Tula Toli, where 4,000 others lived almost identically. They thought little about what lay beyond their village, areas declared "black zones", where the military's siege was enforced. Any regular interaction with the outside world was with the overbearing authorities of their neighbouring village, a small hamlet of ethnic Rakhine, the Buddhist ethnic group who had historically lived alongside the Rohingya in northern Rakhine State but who enjoyed all the power and citizenship. Occasional reminders of the Rohingya's fragility were delivered by the Rakhine administrator or visiting soldiers or on worried whispers that travelled from other Rohingya villages.

Though she and her husband aged and their children grew taller, Momtaz lived as if suspended in time, subsisting long enough to ensure the next generation would do the same. They existed and did little more, unaware that a storm was gathering over northern Rakhine. Of course, there had been signs—arrests, army raids, yet more restrictions on movement—but they were hard to distinguish from the disturbances the Rohingya were used to. They had little inkling that a day was approaching that would carve Tula Toli's name into the collective Rohingya memory and sear it on the bodies of survivors. The Tatmadaw was coming to crush their quiet forever.

* * *

In August 2017, the military returned to Rakhine State in full force, with a rage that reminded older Rohingya generations of why they had accepted lives of acquiescence. They tore through villages, burning homes and shooting wildly but with purpose, sending their populations eastwards to Bangladesh. Tula Toli lay on the way, a stopping point for the Rohingya who had crossed over from the other side of the Mayu mountains, their villages already purged. Over several days, a colony of the terrified began to grow on the village's perimeter, even joined by survivors from Dual Toli, a nearby Rohingya hamlet whose destruction immediately brought survivors to Tula Toli. Since 25 August, the army claimed it had been responding to an attack by Rohingya militants on border posts that had killed twelve members of the security forces. The Arakan Rohingya Salvation Army (ARSA), in turn, said their attack was "defensive", a response to two weeks of raids that had turned up Rohingya bodies all over the state. "This is a legitimate step for us to defend the world's persecuted people and liberate the oppressed people from the hands of the oppressors!" the group tweeted.

The attack had not been sophisticated, carried out by mobs mostly armed with sticks, knives and a few firearms they had stolen from Burmese soldiers. Myanmar blamed them for the violence that followed, even accusing them of killing other Rohingya and burning their homes, but not long after the 25 August attacks, ARSA faded almost into obscurity. The pattern was an amplified echo of the attack a year earlier that had announced ARSA's presence. On 9 October 2016, ARSA killed nine police officers in simultaneous attacks at three border posts—again, their weapons were knives, slingshots and stolen firearms. The group then practically fell off the map while the Myanmar military carried out "clearance operations" that forced tens of thousands of Rohingya civilians into Bangladesh and built up the tensions that formed the backdrop to the 25 August eruption. As some of the country's most notorious battalions were shipped into Rakhine State, young Rohingya men, who had little idea of who ARSA were, slept in the forests at night to avoid arrest. Stories of young women being raped were so widespread that fathers began sending their daughters alone to Bangladesh. But August's onslaught reached a level the Rohingya had not experienced before. At least 6,700 were killed by the military in the month that followed, according to estimates by Médecins Sans Frontières (MSF). Later, Rohingya volunteers conducting their own survey among refugees in Bangladesh put the number at more than 10,000.

Four days after Rakhine had started burning, the people of Tula Toli were seriously concerned. The violence in Dual Toli, which had carried the sounds and smells of death to their doorsteps, had made it more real and after days of taking in refugees, the villagers were bracing for violence themselves and planning to leave. They were stopped by a man named Aung Ko Sing. He was the chairman, or *ukatta*, of Min Gyi, the collective name for Tula Toli and its neighbouring settlement of ethnic Rakhine Buddhists, who were the majority in Rakhine State as a whole but outnumbered by Rohingya in its north. He was not liked. Though the Rohingya community far outnumbered their Rakhine neighbours, they were not allowed to vote and so had no say in Aung Ko Sing's appointment. They associated him with the military: a man who patrolled Tula Toli when the army was looking for arrests to make, picking out young Rohingya to be consigned to a jail cell only to later accept bribes that secured their release. When Tula Toli's Rohingya were preparing to join the caravan heading west to Bangladesh, Aung Ko Sing told them to wait. They met on the night of 29 August to discuss their fears and he promised, as their *ukatta*, to take responsibility for the safety of his Rohingya neighbours. His promise did not hold beyond that meeting. During the night, a helicopter landed in Min Gyi carrying uniforms and weapons for Rakhine villagers.[1]

Soon after light broke through the darkness, the soldiers and freshly armed villagers marched on Tula Toli from three directions, encircling it at the edges. Though still early, the day had started with its first prayer; already people were in the paddy fields and sitting in shops, still nervous but encouraged by Aung Ko Sing's promise of safety. Children were out playing, unaware that the sound of war was about to break their quiet. The Tatmadaw announced its arrival as it had done in so many Rohingya villages before. First the villagers heard the dull thud of a rocket-propelled grenade being launched, then a moment later the explosion that ate through fragile Rohingya homes. Gunfire immediately crackled through the air, giving just enough warning for those who lived furthest away to grab their families and dart towards the forested hills before the soldiers could block them off. They crawled into the shrubbery and silenced the children, not moving to avoid attracting any attention, forced to watch as the massacre began below.

They saw the soldiers start from the outskirts and tear through the village with the purpose of a planned operation. The first to face the military's fury were those new arrivals sheltered on Tula Toli's edges. They had run through villages and forest and found, this time, there was nowhere left to escape to. Almost half the people who died in Tula Toli on 30 August died there, in that initial assault. The rest were jolted by the initial bombardment, which shook the village out of its homes. The attackers pushed inwards, squeezing the survivors towards the bank of the river that wraps around Tula Toli. One of the few grainy, shaky videos that emerged of that day was filmed from the other side of the river. It showed hundreds of people spread over hundreds of metres, stumbling towards the muddy embankment, exactly where the Tatmadaw wanted them. There the attackers launched another hail of gunfire, thinning out the trapped crowd then purposely lodging bullets in the rest, individually, and swinging machetes at their limbs.

The strong and the desperate chanced the only escape route left to them—the river itself. Some of the fitter men, most of them young but some with enough strength left in their arms, beat back the current to make it to the other side. They crafted rafts from plastic cans and bamboo, floating them across to tow children and elders to safety. Others were carried off by the water, some of them still thrashing away and others lifeless, shot in the back as they swam. The attackers dug pits by the riverbank and filled them with the dead as well as some who were still breathing, bleeding out from severed limbs. They piled bamboo branches and dried paddy crops on top and a helicopter poured gasoline from the sky. Then they set the pit on fire. No one has been allowed to visit Tula Toli since.

Momtaz

Momtaz was sitting in the river's shallows, where she and the other women had been ordered to wait as their husbands were

killed and buried. They had grabbed whichever child was close
and evacuated their homes as soon as they heard the assault
starting, but were quickly trapped between the fury of the soldiers and the river, its current too strong for their children to
traverse. So, she sat there, watching the bullets and the burning.
She watched the soldiers slashing at Rohingya with such fury
and frequency that their long knives became blunt. They wrestled her two youngest sons from her and threw them into the
water. Other women described the same. Some saw babies
chucked directly into fires.[2] Her last son, the eldest, was bludg-
eoned around the head, then hacked and burned there on the
riverbank where they were digging the pits. Momtaz struggled
with them as best she could, but it was useless. The only survivor
was 6-year-old Rozeya, who had tried frantically to pull her dead
brother from the flames engulfing his body. A group of soldiers
hauled them from the water and marched them into Tula Toli's
freshly emptied homes. They did the same with all the remaining
young women. "They dragged me to the home and raped me
there", said Momtaz. "Then another soldier came and tied my
hands and did the same. Then they set the house on fire."

The use of rape in Tula Toli, and in all of the Rohingya villages that were emptied during those weeks from 25 August, was
described by Human Rights Watch as "methodical". But there is
no precise word the Rohingya use for this crime they fear almost
as much as death. Momtaz and other women from Tula Toli
spoke of the *zulum* that happened inside those burning homes.
Literally, it translates as "oppression", but what they describe
reveals their meaning. It was the same story echoed by Rohingya
women from across northern Rakhine, women who had never
met each other but were connected by family lost and trauma
gained—by the moment they blacked out in pain. When Momtaz
awoke, it was to flames that had started biting at her face and had
seared the right-hand side of her body. Rozeya was bleeding

from where a soldier's machete blows had struck her skull. They were both lying in a pile of bodies. For the first time that day, there were no soldiers waiting to pounce and yet death seemed more inevitable than ever. Then Rozeya spotted the hole in the wall. Momtaz lifted the limp arm that had been resting on her and the two finally crawled to their escape in a vegetable patch outside the home. They dragged themselves just far enough to escape the fire's heat and crouched in the greenery, afraid to move before the soldiers had left. Momtaz could only imagine what had happened to the rest of her family; she could not know for sure. She certainly could not go looking for them. She had seen the riverbank: her neighbours shot and hacked at, the women led away, the fires lit on barricaded homes. Her mother and sisters, surely, were dead. So, she did not risk the life of her last child by leaving that vegetable patch. Bleeding and scared, the two of them waited for the darkness that would end the day. Then, like everyone who escaped, they sneaked into the forest, barely alive.

Anwara

Though little more than a decade and a kilometre separated Anwara Begum from Momtaz, life had already tossed her far beyond their village tract. Twice she had been one of those Rohingya who had marched towards Bangladesh, and twice she had been returned on a boat to the country she had been told had returned to peace. She had promised herself she would never do it again. She did not want to return to the bitter memories that Bangladesh held for her. For twenty-five years, she had kept that oath, keeping her head down and bearing the hardships and humiliation of Myanmar, because it was better to be home than to live as a stranger. But she knew that could not continue when she saw clouds of red forming in the river.

TULA TOLI

By the time the Tatmadaw arrived in Tula Toli, Anwara and her family had already spent five days in the forest, under the rain, swarmed by insects and pulling leeches off their bodies. They sneaked back to their homes at night to feed their children and sleep, when they were sure the military would not come. They had returned to their hiding place in the bushes on the morning of the Tula Toli massacre when the smell of smoke began streaming over to Wykhong, their village slightly north of Tula Toli, on the other side of the river. When time did not mute the sounds of violence, they shuffled over to the river to see what was happening. Anwara saw its waters weighed down with the consequences—bodies mutilated or simply drowned in their attempt to escape. Dead babies were being washed up on the riverbank. Hiding was suddenly not a priority. Tula Toli's escapees had crafted rafts to tow the elderly and children to safety, but the hands Anwara's husband Ruhul Amin were now clasping were already drained of life.

Ruhul and his brother, a local imam, had instinctively started plucking bodies from the water. In their hearts, they wanted to read them their Islamic rites, a last act of duty for souls brutally hacked from their bodies. But with each body they retrieved, the weight of their task grew as heavy on their minds as it did on their arms. By the time they had pulled eight people from the river, they began to realise the overwhelming scale of their task. The river was still bloated with Rohingya death. They would be stuck there all day, forever plunging their hands into the water but unable to dig a single grave before the soldiers finished with Tula Toli and came for them as well. Resigned, Ruhul turned to his brother: "We can't bury them and if we leave them here they will just become prey for the animals. It's better for them in the water."

They left the river and, once again, left their homes. This time they had no intention of waiting in the jungle. There was almost no chance of them surviving if they stayed where they were—everyone who had tried to stand their ground, even those who simply took a break from running, was eventually caught by the Tatmadaw. So Anwara and her family followed the others, not consciously deciding to return to the country she had sworn never to return to, but aware that she was on a path she had trodden before. It took three days in the rain. They crept through more forests during the day and stopped at night in villages already abandoned, taking shelter under the roofs of homes that had not been entirely destroyed.

Though they did not know the exact route, they continued to stumble westwards until they reached the River Naf, the border between Myanmar and Bangladesh. It seemed as if the whole Rohingya nation had gathered there on the riverbank, ready to abandon the homeland they were told they did not belong to. Though the river was far wider than the tributary beside Tula Toli, some young men swam themselves to safety. Others crafted emergency rafts from bamboo and jerry cans, the same types they had used already to escape and to retrieve the dead. The rest relied on the lines of boatmen who had arrived on the Naf's eastern bank—many of them from Bangladesh, compelled by a sense of duty after seeing the smoke, others by the sense that money could be made. Anwara handed over the gold she had managed to take from her home before she left, worth 240,000 Burmese kyat (US$200), to pay for a ride to Bangladesh. Anyone who had left empty-handed had to wait on a boatman's mercy.

* * *

Tula Toli's survivors were emerging in Bangladesh by the day of Eid-ul-Adha. It should have been a day of festivities, but for all the arriving Rohingya it became the reference point that helped them to calculate exactly when they joined the long, painful stumble across the border. Those who did not come by boat had walked to the north of the Naf, across paddy fields made swamp-like in the recent monsoon. They balanced on the small strips of land between fields crumbling from the unexpected footfall. Some carried belongings and many had children or their elderly strapped to their backs. A few brought their dead with them, their slumped bodies requiring two people to carry them, one holding their legs and the other their torso, struggling to provide a final dignity to their lost relatives. The Bangladeshis who had seen smoke rising from across the border now watched death land on their doorsteps. Boats that tried to arrive through the Bay of Bengal capsized in the sea and hundreds died of injuries and illness en route. The locals rushed to the border to provide food and water. Many offered their homes as refuge. Bangladeshi NGOs joined, giving first aid to the tired and taking the injured to hospital. The army helped carry the weakest, and journalists documented their staggering arrival. They asked what had happened and heard stories, often shared horrors, from across northern Rakhine. It was Tula Toli, with the sing-song cadence to its name and brutal story, that began to stick in their minds.

Momtaz and Rozeya arrived there unconscious, carried by one of their neighbours, who had found them hiding once the soldiers moved on from Tula Toli. They were taken to the MSF hospital in Kutupalong, where doctors stitched up Rozeya's head and treated and dressed Momtaz's burns. Many of the other women with her in hospital were survivors from Tula Toli as well. They were released together after weeks in hospital, stepping into the stormy night heavily bandaged and with no home to go to.

* * *

Around 40km south of Tula Toli is a village called Kiladaung. Before August 2017, it was the village whose fate was freshest in Rohingya minds. The UN confirmed at least forty-eight

Rohingya were killed by security forces and Rakhine civilians on 14 January 2014, although some Rohingya believed bodies had been buried to conceal the real number, which they thought was more likely to be in the hundreds. MSF reported that they had treated twenty-two patients from the village after the attack and then been banned from providing services in the country. The village was cordoned off and Myanmar set up its own investigation—its conclusion was that reports of a massacre were false and the burning of Rohingya homes may have been the work of "entities with political motivation". Whatever story the government tried to officially sell about Kiladaung, it had its own local impact in Maungdaw State's villages. For many, it was the realisation of their fear that intercommunal riots of the kind that had ravaged the Rohingya community in the state's capital Sittwe in 2012 would reach rural Rakhine. It was a spectre that had hung over Tula Toli as well. Rakhine village administrators had repeatedly threatened their Rohingya neighbours with another Kiladaung to get what they wanted. Its horrors were wielded when they refused to sign up for National Verification Cards (NVC), an identity document usually given to foreigners and which Rohingya feared would cement their status, in the eyes of the state, as outsiders infiltrating from Bangladesh.

But now every village was a Kiladaung, their dead killed in mass executions and buried in collective graves or thrown into rivers. Their homes had been burned and the army claimed it was sabotage, borrowing all the tactics it used in that one village and replicating them on a mass scale to form a military operation more coordinated and aggressive than those of previous decades. In the past, many had run in fear of the violence they anticipated, while others had sat it out, even as Tatmadaw violence increased and their restrictions on Rohingya life grew more pervasive. In August 2017, it all coalesced into the single storm that wiped the Rohingya almost entirely from Rakhine State.

Ming Gyi's *ukatta*, Aung Ko Sing, had also told the Rohingya that they would be another Kiladaung. When the time came, the violence he orchestrated was far worse, killing hundreds and completely cleansing the area of its Rohingya populations. The chars and scars of Tula Toli are all that remain of a village that had housed 4,300 Rohingya. Myanmar does not allow visitors but satellites can still see the ghost town, which stands out from the surrounding greenery with its strange red tinge. To investigate the violence, a UN fact-finding mission had to rely on satellite images and interviews with Rohingya, declaring a year afterwards that Myanmar's so-called clearance operations were fuelled by "genocidal intent".[3] Human Rights Watch said the events of 30 August 2017 showed signs of military planning.[4] The Rohingya included their allegations against the village administration as part of that plan—they believe the *ukatta*'s promises of safety were only ever designed to lure them into a false sense of security. And there is evidence that the entire operation was planned, not simply a reaction to ARSA as claimed.

In early August, the 33rd and 99th Light Infantry Divisions moved into Rakhine State. The battalions were already notorious for their violence and alleged human rights abuses, and when the 33rd returned to the front against Kachin rebels in 2018 new animosity was breathed into that conflict. The UN report said their presence in Tula Toli had unofficially been confirmed, backed by sightings on the day of soldiers dressed similarly to the rest but in helmets.

"We will clear out their villages", a soldier repeated, again and again, in a video[5] obtained by rights group Fortify Rights, apparently showing a soldier talking to a group of Rakhine villagers before 25 August. "We're going to crack down on them, severely and fast", he said. "If you see they are fleeing, we should be very happy about that."

2

THE RIVER NAF

Nobi (May 2015)

"Are you going there?" Nobi stammers as his legs snap stiff, his body recoiling in a cry to be far from the river his parents crossed with him when he was a young child in 1991 and they ran from their home.

It's not that he fears the River Naf, exactly, though the history of that waterway would have justified it. Cleaving the border between Bangladesh and Myanmar, for decades it has seen survivors seek safety through the flooded paddy fields to its north or on Bangladesh's coastline further south, where the river meets the wild waters of the Bay of Bengal. The river has itself borne hundreds of thousands more, through storms that toss panicked souls already struggling to cling to the vessels, both boat and body, that carry them.

As he ambles absentmindedly towards its banks, it is not any collective Rohingya memory of the role the River Naf played in his community's exile that strikes Nobi with fear. It is because that river is a place where men wear uniforms. We are meeting for the first time and he is, in that moment, describing to me the terror of a childhood squeezed between the fingers of the Bangladeshi army's closed fist, assigned to remind him he was not native to the country he lived in, just as Burmese soldiers had earlier harassed his parents to leave the country both they and their grandparents were born in. Everything about him is new to me—he is the first Rohingya I have truly met, for an open conversation rather than one guided by questions. But it is in watching, rather than listening, that I learn most. He is a kind man and though his face is young it is also tired. He is nervous and his eyes are watchful, forever darting around, scanning his environment, even though there is no one there. The reason, then, that he has suddenly frozen like a troubled deer is that he has spotted a group of uniformed men stepping down to the river's bank. They are marshalling some men, who look ragged and tired, stumbling along in single file, dressed in worn shirts and wrapped from the waist down in *lungis*. The uniforms do not belong to police, as Nobi at first fears, but to coastguard officers more interested in the men they are bringing to land: trafficking victims who have recently jumped from a people smuggler's fishing trawler into the sea.

"They might interrogate me. You know, I don't have a national ID card of this country, so they will ask me why I am here", says Nobi. He is 28, a man questioning his own right to be anywhere beyond the refugee camp he was raised in, let alone the homeland he was born in on the other side of the water. He has learned this over the course of his life. I have to go and investigate, but he decides to retreat and promises to wait in another location out of eyesight so we can continue talking.

Nobi is not the first Rohingya to be struck by a special fear at the sight of a uniformed man. They are the visible presence of the state over a stateless people, a community without reason to feel any of the patriotism, typical of most nations, towards men armed and uniformed. Whether from the army or navy, coast-guard or paramilitaries, or whether that cloth sits on Burmese or Bangladeshi shoulders, none of it belongs to them. The Tatmadaw uniform represents a nation they have been told for almost forty years they do not belong to. It was worn by those who came to their villages with guns and machetes and with fuel to burn their homes down. Men in Burmese military uniforms took Rohingya men for forced labour, raped Rohingya women and told them to leave the country—pointing to Bangladesh. Across the border, more men, now wearing Bangladeshi uniforms, policed their lives in squalid refugee camps and beat them till the time came to round up the Rohingya and pack them on boats across the river back to Myanmar. Though it got worse in later years, they had been bounced back and forth since shortly after independence. "The East Bengal Government, says a message from Dacca, has closed the east Pakistan-Burma border to prevent refugees entering from Arakan", read a short report by *The Times* on 2 February 1949, when present-day Bangladesh was still part of Pakistan. "Large numbers of Muslim refugees are understood to have crossed the frontier after recent rioting between Muslims and Burmese." In October 1959, the Associated Press reported that 10,000 Muslims had fled "from Buddhist Burma to Moslem East Pakistan".

The same stories occasionally appeared over a few lines in the columns of western newspapers during the decade between these two news reports. The victims were rounded up by Burmese soldiers and told to leave the country. Then, after a week or two camped out along the border, they were forced to return. The Rohingya position in Myanmar was not entirely settled after Burma's independence and the Second World War. Resentment remained after the British and Japanese, fighting for control of Rakhine State, pitted Muslims against Buddhists. When the British departed and partitioned India along religious lines, newly

19

independent Burma found Muslim East Pakistan sitting next door—a neighbour some Rohingya had wanted to join. Instead of a new harmony, they faced the challenge of nation-building among multi-ethnic populations who were often unhappy about the new borders. Pakistan was soon facing the rights movement that ultimately led to Bangladesh's independence, while the Burmese government was immediately confronted with an insurgency in Karen State and smaller rebellions from Rakhine and Chin. Some Rohingya believed they had been promised independence by the British in exchange for fighting the Japanese and took up arms to fight for it, calling themselves the Mujahideen. They engaged the Burmese army in small skirmishes and little more, but it was enough to bring the Burmese army bearing down on Rohingya villages on the frontier, searching for guerillas and collaborators.

The stories Western newspapers reported from the borders were essentially the same ones that would crop up frequently in the future: of the Rohingya as illegal interlopers, questions about their nationality and loyalties, and attacks by their Rakhine neighbours. The Mujahideen were a fringe group who had only tenuous links to the community and achieved little, yet still dominated headlines and diplomacy. Burmese generals frequently asked their Pakistani counterparts to clamp down on any Mujahideen fugitives on the other side of the border. Rohingya villagers suffered from these operations, but overall it was still a time before the worst came, when the Rohingya were citizens described by the country's first post-independence prime minister, U Nu, as "national brethren", and Rohingya-language broadcasts aired on state radio. General Ne Win's military coup in 1962 changed that. He discarded some of the more harmonious ideas of the country's founders and began shaping a nationalistic identity that had no time for identities that belonged to the country's frontiers, whether they were Karen, Kachin, Chin or Rohingya.

By 1978, the Rohingya were a major target for General Ne Win when reshaping the country's identity. His army launched Operation Nagamin (Operation Dragon King), forcing 200,000 from their homes with unprecedented ferocity. Myanmar's military regime insisted the operation was simply a way to screen foreigners in Rakhine and that the Rohingya exodus was proof they did not belong. In the document signed when Myanmar agreed to take them back from Bangladesh that same year, the refugees were described as "lawful residents of Burma". By 1982 that was no longer the case; when the new Citizenship Law listed 135 ethnic groups settled in the country before the British occupation of 1824, the Rohingya were not among them. When another round of Rohingya flight and displacement came in 1991, and continued throughout most of that decade, the roughly 250,000 escapees were leaving an atmosphere created by Operation Nagamin and their subsequent loss of citizenship. Their freedoms had been curtailed and their policed lives were subject to the whims of an ever-present military who established a regime of forced labour.

On both occasions, Bangladesh forced most back with repatriations that spared only a few. However, the situation had deteriorated so much by the 1990s that even as Bangladeshi boats carried Rohingya eastwards across the Naf, more refugees were arriving. The flow never really stopped, but its intensity would increase with Rakhine's ruptures; localised massacres and intercommunal riots would once again load the Naf with Rohingya bodies. Some tried to escape beyond Bangladesh to avoid being once more bounced between nations that did not want them, but they found their statelessness followed them wherever they sought some measure of security and freedom. Whichever route they took, others found ways to exploit their desperation for profit.

The Rohingya have run from the Burmese troops who kill them to their Bangladeshi counterparts who have policed their lives in a different way, looming over them in their exile then turning the screw when governments decide they need to return to Myanmar. The same was true of the Pakistani government before Bangladesh's birth. Whenever the Rohingya have tired of their lives in camps in either of these countries, they have turned to trafficking networks to be smuggled abroad, only to encounter other uniforms in new places—worn by people who profit from, or even manage, the criminal rings or the immigration police whom they have, as undocumented migrants, learned to fear.

* * *

As buses heading to the southernmost tip of Bangladesh pull aside to pick up passengers at the last crossroads out of Cox's Bazar, the slipshod resort town Bangladesh views as its main tourist attraction, a boy jumps aboard with a basket full of fried chilli snacks. He hands out the *jhal bora* in small parcels of newspaper, for a payment of pennies. Outside, lorries swaying under their load of bamboo poles or rice in bags labelled "Export of Myanmar" rattle through the junction on their way to supply the Rohingya refugee camps. They breeze past a dust-layered white sign announcing the "Arakan Road". Now known as the Cox's Bazar-Teknaf Highway, after the southern town it links to, much of the road's nature and purpose is linked to Rakhine State, historically known as Arakan. For more than 90km the road runs more or less parallel to the border, at points revealing to passengers the Mayu mountains rising beyond the other side of the Naf. Even the dozens of checkpoints in place to stop Rohingya refugees from leaving the camps for Bangladesh's main towns, or to stifle the movement of drugs smuggled from Myanmar, tell of this rural road's persisting international heritage. It is a reminder of a history that connected the river's two banks long before any Rohingya crossed it in fear and one that does not chime with Myanmar's official narrative: that the Rohingya are recent

"Bengali" intruders: Muslims pushing eastwards to overwhelm Buddhism, with no historical link to Rakhine.

Cox's Bazar district and Teknaf to the south are littered with evidence of a history that does not fit within the boundaries of nation states. It may seem on first inspection that the region's one-lane rural highways resemble any other in the country, lined with paddy fields and cutting sporadically through the centres of villages where gaggles of primly uniformed children seem perpetually on their way to or from school. But there is also the occasional Rakhine village where, instead of mosques, temples stand proud and groups of orange-robed monks alight from autorickshaws outside monasteries. In a corner of Cox's Bazar town, a government school for the Rakhine community teaches in their native language and every so often a home boasting Rakhine architecture stands apart from the mass of decaying concrete apartment blocks. Inside homes, colourful Buddhist shrines adorn painted plaster walls alongside portraits of sons in Bangladeshi military uniforms. The Rohingya have clear ethnic, religious and linguistic links with Bengalis in Cox's Bazar and the wider Chittagong area, but Rakhine life similarly spans the banks of the Naf, reaching into modern Bangladesh where they live with full citizenship, unlike the Rohingya.

Myanmar's official history of the Rohingya in Rakhine State tells a more cut-and-dried story, one that begins only with the British, the colonisers who brought Bengalis across the river to work the local paddy fields. There were no Rohingya before, the story says. It was true that the British did bring workers, even building a rail line to transport them, but not necessarily that those workers settled in the region when the season's work ended. There is, however, record of a Rohingya presence far older than the British Empire's. The border that stretched along the River Naf when Britain granted Burma independence in 1948 was not the resumption of some pre-colonial constant—those boundaries had always been much more fluid when the powers of the day were the Arakan Kingdom and the Bengal Sultanate (and later the Mughal Empire it was absorbed into). In fact, the Burmese Kingdom's own sovereignty over Rakhine was not as perennial as is assumed in its modern narrative. It only overcame a weakened Arakan Kingdom in 1785, less than forty years before the British then took the region during the First Anglo-Burmese War. That war was in part prompted by British harbouring of Arakanese rebels, whose desire for independence has lived on in the ethnic Rakhine.

That rebellious sense of Rakhine individualism remains strong in Cox's Bazar, where local Rakhine refer to a man named Maung Di as the "professor" of their history. This Bangladeshi civil servant lives in the centre of the town, in an apartment filled with the histories he's written of a Rakhine heritage he sees as distinct from both Bengal and Burma. In fact, the history of the town he lives in is very much wrapped up with the group's rejection of Bamar rule. He says it was named after Captain Hiram Cox, an East India Company officer sent to deal with the Rakhine refugee crisis at the turn of the nineteenth century.

"It was the same thing happening now but 250 years earlier", he says, describing the thousands of Rakhines who fled Burmese rule to Cox's Bazar, known then as Palongkali.

Such mass shifts of people were common before British rule, when there was a history of pull and push between neighbouring Bengal and Arakan. If they were not at war, they traded and occasionally became embroiled in the intrigues of each other's royal courts. When Arakanese King Min Saw Mon was deposed and forced to flee his kingdom by the armies of the neighbouring Kingdom of Ava in 1404, it was with the Sultan of Bengal Jalaluddin Muhammad Shah that he sought refuge, entering his service as a military commander. In Bengal's then capital Gaur, he built rank and trust until the sultan eventually agreed to support Saw Mon's bid to retake the Arakan Kingdom with an army of "Afghan adventurers".[1] The first attempt failed when one of his commanders betrayed him, but he regrouped and on the second try Saw Mon succeeded in restoring his kingdom, marking the victory soon afterwards by founding Mrauk-U, a new Arakan capital that would remain until the kingdom was dissolved with the Burmese invasion in 1785. As a condition of his relationship with the sultan, Saw Mon's kingdom became a vassal state of Bengal until 1531, a period when the various kings of Arakan would take on Muslim titles and mint coins with the Islamic declaration of faith.[2]

But throughout this time, the Arakanese Kingdom in Mrauk-U grew stronger and increasingly independent of Bengal. When the Portuguese arrived in the sixteenth century, they developed a partnership that helped Arakan eat into Bengali territory, which by then had become part of the Mughal Empire. They took Ramu, essentially where the modern Rohingya refugee camps lie on the other side of the River Naf, and by 1578 had wrestled control of Chittagong, the crucial port city close to the heart of Bengal. Arakanese and Portuguese pirates raided the Bengali coast to kidnap slaves, many of them Bengali Muslims, and sell them in the Mrauk-U markets to local dignitaries or the Dutch East India Company, who from 1624 to 1665 took more than 11,000 slaves from Arakan to modern-day Jakarta.[3]

By 1660, the roles had reversed and it was Mughal Prince Muhammad Shah Shuja fleeing Bengal to Arakan after infighting with his own siblings.[4] With his soldiers, family and riches, he set sail from Dhaka and was given refuge by Arakan King Sanda Thudama. He lived for a while in Arakan, hoping to be given a fleet of ships to take him to Mecca, but was ultimately killed there in unclear circumstances. There were rumours that Shuja refused the king's proposal to marry his daughter and a failed attempt to take the Arakan Kingdom for himself. The

Mughal Emperor Aurangzeb, whom Shuja had fled, decided to avenge the death of his brother in a foreign kingdom by sending Shaista Khan, a Bengal-based general in the Mughal army. His 300 warships and land force of 6,500 soldiers quickly took back Chittagong and stormed eastwards, driving the Arakanese out of strongholds on Sandwip island and Ramu and re-establishing the eastern frontier with the Arakan Kingdom.

Amid this movement of armies and borders, there remained an exceptional diversity among the populations of this disputed territory between Mrauk-U and Chittagong. Both were cosmopolitan—Chittagong because it was a major port city in the Bay of Bengal that attracted seafarers and traders, and Mrauk-U as a place where the Arakanese Kingdom's interactions with neighbouring Burma and Bengal were reflected within its courts. If anything, the conquest and piracy brought new people to Mrauk-U who would add to its heritage. To this day, Arakan's Kaman Muslims, distinct from the Rohingya, are considered descendants of Shuja's bowmen who were conscripted into the Arakan bodyguard after he was killed.[5] It also brought to its courts the famed poet Syed Alaol, who ended up in Arakan after he and his father were caught up in a slavers' raid in the Bay of Bengal. In a royal court abundant with Muslim advisors, Persian was a common medium for the poetry produced within, but Alaol worked in Bengali as well, not only sealing his legacy as one of the language's pioneers of poetry but also leaving a cultural mark on a region that Myanmar would later present as having only a singular culture.

This history of the movement of people and cultures across the River Naf sits awkwardly with Myanmar's official version that the Rohingya have only recently crossed from Bangladesh. In a world where the boundary it served was fluid, the narrow river was only the slightest of barriers against movement. The sea to the south brought even more connection with Arab traders from much further afield. Rohingya histories, largely based on the Rakhine-based Rohingya historian U Ba Tha who was prominent in the 1960s, draw on these stories for their explanation of Rohingya identity and how they are distinct from their neighbours in Chittagong. The Rohingya language, U Ba Tha explained, is a mixture of Bengali, Arabic, Urdu, Persian and Arakanese, created by this experience.

"Many Arakanese of Akyab District [Sittwe] are shouting at the top of their voice that these Muslims are Chittagonians or Kalas as they are similar to the East Pakistanis in appearance; but they are distinct in habit, culture, dress, name, and dialect," he wrote in the *Rangoon Guardian* in 1960.[6]

Decades later, these same thoughts would harass Nobi as he sat atop the hills behind Nayapara, his home for more than two decades. He and other Rohingya often climb these green hills to stare into the vista of a country they cannot remember leaving. In the foreground sit the Bangladeshi paddy fields on the river's western bank. Then, as they cast their eyes upwards, the trees of Myanmar lie only a couple of kilometres away. In the distance, the Mayu mountains stand tall over Rakhine, a Rohingya's visual guide to how distant home is. This view was less serene during the manic months of 2017. Bangladeshi photographer Masfiqur Sohan caught one of the most iconic photos of that time—a group of Rohingya gather on one of those hills behind Nayapara, looking out into the distance where, just beyond the Naf, clouds of smoke billow above the wreckage of another Rohingya village demolished by the Myanmar military.

On their phones, Nobi and other young Rohingya born or raised in Bangladesh saw what lay behind the wall of smoke. The pictures coming through on social media were of faces bloodied and bodies lying limp in the grass. When they rushed down to the river, too impassioned to fear approaching it any more, they found the remnants of the Rohingya population stumbling across—including members of their own families they had not met for decades, if ever. Nobi personally brought 100 families over to Nayapara and sheltered them in a school he had built for the young Rohingya he privately tutored. He fed them and had them treated by some of the camp's homegrown informal medics.

In a small room, he cooked for them with donations from the existing community and found places for them to sleep. But when it came time to think about what had happened, how this home he had lived in as a minority was now becoming the holding place for almost the entirety of the Rohingya nation, he turned to Facebook. One day, his exasperation became more philosophical than the usual questions about why the Rohingya were left helpless. Turning to that river he had frozen beside in fear when we first met in 2015, he echoed U Ba Tha's frustrations about who the Rohingya are in the eyes of their neighbours.

"When a small minority group is [on the] eastern side of this river, they are called Bengali Kola by the Burmese people", Nobi wrote, noting the racial slur some Burmese use against Rohingya in reference to their darker skin. "When they are [on the] western side of this river they are called Burmaya.

"No peace, no dignity, no state, no happiness, no justice, no hope and no home for them still in any corners of this world."

3

THE ESCAPE VALVE

Shob Mehraj (1970s)

At first, there was no government. Shob Mehraj remembers only the village council, which dealt with minor matters and disputes, and the times a government could have helped her village cope with its deaths and disasters. She remembers losing her mother to illness when she was young and no help arriving, no hospital they could access and no record that her mother's mark on the world had been smudged away. Rohingya life existed only for the people around it, until it did not. She remembers when the government did come, much later, in the form of soldiers dressed in military fatigues, not civil servants or teachers or doctors. But when she was a child, there was no manifestation of that central state, the Union of Burma, in her version of northern Rakhine. It had not, yet, found her village. The memories Shob Mehraj has of that Burma have faded with her three decades as a refugee, spent in a hut that has changed little since she arrived in Bangladesh save for the addition of tin-sheet roofing to guard against the rain and the empty spaces that have replaced a husband who passed away and children who married and moved out. But there are moments that cling to her mind.

She remembers a large boat; a boat that reminds her that the government was never there. It arrived, capsized, with a storm that flooded the village, tearing down the trees and inundating their homes. This all happened at some point in her childhood, though she cannot pinpoint exactly when because she cannot remember her age. Most Rohingya never had their births recorded and, deprived of a conventional education (through either neglect or conspiracy), some are unaware of the year's months. When spent in refugee camps, those months all blend into each other anyway. Still, when she pauses for a moment and guesses at 90, the estimate *does* surprise—her daughter Anu is only 19 years old. The Gregorian calendar matters little to the Rakhine countryside or a Bangladeshi camp. Shob Mehraj *feels* 90.

When the cyclone destroyed her home, Shob Mehraj and her family went to stay at another family's home, but soon theirs was gone too. Not a single home was spared in the end. Every form of shelter blown away, the families could only huddle together under the trees and wait for the rain to stop. As they waited for the rain to go and for the government to come, the villagers scavenged from the abandoned ship, living off puffed rice that had been stored as an instant and non-perishable fuel for its crew. They waited until the cyclone finally did move on and they could return to the wreckage of their homes and begin the rebuild no one was going to help with. This was the cycle Shob Mehraj remembered when she was young; of quiet neglect in their ignored corner of Rakhine. They lived, survived and died without passing through the thoughts of the central state. There was no violence yet because there they were forgotten, hardly a concern in a Rakhine that was underdeveloped; a place physically isolated from the rest of the country because of its mountainous perimeter; and where investment in its poor road, infrastructure and electricity networks was neglected. The experience was not typical of every Rohingya village—the military had, of course, been expelling Rohingya since the 1940s—but it was also not rare.

Maung Kyaw Nu

As a community, the Rohingya were on the peripheries of the Union of Burma, but they did not yet feel hated. Not all lived in peace but most recollect quiet, uneventful lives where neither army nor government featured heavily. Since independence there had been a weekly hour of Rohingya-language radio aired by the state broadcaster, split between Qur'an recital and news bulletins voiced by Rohingya who lived in the capital, then known as Rangoon.[1] The city's universities and Islamic religious seminaries could still easily count Rohingya among their students, and Rangoon University had a Rohingya Students Association. At the opposite end of the scale to Shob Mehraj were the Rohingya middle class—like Maung Kyaw Nu, a man of means who studied at the prestigious university in Mandalay and received a student discount on his airfare. He studied and moved freely, taking with him the wife and children he had from a very early arranged marriage. He used a Burmese name to blend into society, instead of the Rohingya Nazmul Alam. Only in 1974 would he brush with the authorities. Even then, it had nothing to do with being Rohingya.

That November, the death of former UN Secretary-General U Thant sparked a crisis that pitted the government against much of the population, including the Rohingya who moved in student and civil society circles. They were angered when the revered politician's body was returned to Myanmar and found a cold reception from the government, not given the respect and ceremony customary for such an important national figure. Worse

31

than that, he was denied a state funeral. Maung Kyaw Nu was one of a number of students who hatched a plan in protest. They seized the body and marched it to the Rangoon Arts and Sciences University for their own memorial services, forcing the government to act even though it had preferred to downplay U Thant's death. The showdown led to crisis talks, and the government eventually agreed with U Thant's family to bury his body by the revered gilded stupa at Shwedagon Pagoda. But a more radical wing of the student movement was still adamant on following through with their own plans. They seized the body again as it was being readied for burial and took it to another campus draped in the UN flag.

After five days of protest, the wrath of the security forces arrived at what had become almost a revolutionary camp. The police fired tear gas at the students and beat them with baton charges, arresting thousands and setting off riots around Rangoon in reaction to the police brutality. Maung Kyaw Nu was caught up in the crackdown and ended up in prison for the first time, as part of this pan-Burma, pro-democracy movement—as a Burmese student rather than a Rohingya. He was no leader of the movement, simply a member who, confident and eloquent as he was, did not shy away from speaking to the crowds or speaking to the media. That earned him his first stay in jail and would later mark his name. In the short-term, however, his imprisonment was temporary and he was soon released and returned to an ordinary life with the small family waiting for him in Mandalay.

* * *

A telegraph summoned Maung Kyaw Nu to return to Rakhine. It was from his family. His mother was sick. Immediately, he boarded a plane to Sittwe and then took a colonial-era steamer that meandered from the state capital through Rakhine's internal rivers up to Buthidaung. From there, he travelled by land to his village in Maungdaw, the closest district to Bangladesh. The route home was long and circuitous, but the only option for any Rohingya from Maungdaw who had ever been struck by the ambition to travel to Sittwe or Myanmar's interior. It was the type of journey that gnawed through the day and, inevitably, the time came when some of Maung Kyaw Nu's fellow Rohingya wanted to pray. They congregated on the roof of the boat, lining up behind the prayer's designated leader, who recited aloud the passages of the Qur'an, attracting the attention of some of the other travellers. Stirred by the sight, a group of hostile Rakhine passengers formed a circle and began shouting abuse at the worshippers who continued to bow and prostrate themselves, eyes fixed on the places where their foreheads kissed the floor, trying to tune out the noise. But the words they were met with were more than enough to trouble their focus. Maung Kyaw Nu had not been praying but saw another Rohingya had started to mediate, trying to convince the Rakhine to back off. Maung Kyaw Nu asked the man what had happened and immediately became incensed by the affront. "If I shouted at a Buddhist monk", he fired back at the aggressors. "If I said fuck this Buddhist monk, how would you feel? Why do you insult our religion?" The men backed off.

His response was both brave and abrasive, and he delivered those words at maybe the last possible time he could ever do so without weighty consequence. A year later, the social and political landscape of Rakhine began a radical transformation that cemented notions of the Rohingya as alien and enemy. But back then, nothing happened. To Maung Kyaw Nu, this was Rohingya life before 1978's Operation Nagamin, the moment he realised it had all changed, when the Rohingya were not immune from abuse and discrimination from other majority communities. But there was no inkling of the genocide to come. Years later, hindsight would help him understand the landscape had already been altered.

Under the leadership of Prime Minister U Nu, who held the position for most of the country's history between independence and military rule, the Rohingya had already come to know the quelling force of soldiers who were already arriving in villages that were not Shob Mehraj's or Maung Kyaw Nu's. Villages were accused of being linked to the Mujahideen, a band of Rohingya fighters who demanded the autonomous zone promised by the British but which had never been delivered, and who were often victim to sweeping arrest raids and even expulsion to East Pakistan. Few Rohingya identified with the fight and, with the army already fighting insurgencies against the Karen and Shan, not everyone considered it a targeted campaign against the community. When groups of Mujahideen surrendered, they were paraded in the local village grounds and everyone was told to come out and celebrate a step towards peace. The Rohingya were not named as one of Burma's indigenous groups and they were not treated equally, especially as they lived in a frontier region under special military authority, but they were also not existentially threatened. U Nu had, after all, been the one who had described the Rohingya as part of Burma's fraternity.

However, he was overthrown by a military coup in 1962. His usurper, General Ne Win, immediately crushed a federalist movement and, over time, took to fighting the country's many minorities, especially those he saw as a threat to Bamar power or unity. The hour of state radio given to the Rohingya was gone by the late 1960s and Rohingya needed permits to travel, even to Sittwe. Jobs were harder to find and Rohingya in the military, some of whom held senior roles, were expelled. A Rohingya elite in universities, the army and parliament that had persisted since independence started to fade from public life, even if it did not yet die.

All of this had not yet registered with Maung Kyaw Nu who, disconnected from most of his community, still enjoyed the freedoms and privilege of his student bubble. That changed shortly after he made the journey home to visit his sick mother, when some other young Rohingya urged him to travel with them to a nearby forest. What he was faced with was an encampment of Rohingya who had crossed the mountains between Buthidaung and Maungdaw and were talking about going to Bangladesh. They were already tired, scared and hungry. The little rice they had hauled with them was running out. They spoke about villages cleared by the army, even burned to the ground, and women harassed by the government's soldiers. "This is disgusting, I've never heard of this kind of thing", Maung Kyaw Nu said to his friends, incredulous. "We are the same people, why are they doing this?"

Mustak Ahmed

On 6 February 1978, the government announced that it had arrived for the Rohingya. The declaration of their sudden interest in the community as a whole was made in Sittwe with a sea of uniforms of every type: army, police, border guard. Suddenly, they roamed every street of the state capital, checking paperwork and sweeping up the Rohingya who had ventured beyond their villages without the state's permission. They searched for the Rohingya by looking into people's faces, scanning for those apparently Bengali characteristics that betrayed them as foreigners. Any whose facial features evaded their prejudices—the differences between Rohingya and Rakhine were not always so obvious—were able to escape. Those Rohingya who *were* stopped were detained. The questions came later. They were rounded up on the street and marched to a warehouse usually used by a local business for storing fertiliser, but commandeered by officers for their interrogations. Hands bound, the detained Rohingya sat on its dusty floor, each waiting their turn to be hauled in front of an officer sitting among the lines of desks they had set up. They were asked where they were from and to prove it. Some were arrested and some were set free. None really understood what was happening. Operation Nagamin was, ostensibly, a census ordered by Ne Win, but it was no simple exercise in counting the population. The Nagamin the operation was named after are the "Dragon King" figures placed as guards at the entrance to Buddhist temples, safeguarding against intruders. The operation's guiding principle was to weed out the Rohingya who, according to the government, were infiltrators from Bangladesh. Those Rohingya huddled in warehouses were not simply counted as unregistered; the paperless were imprisoned. There were even rumours that one group was thrown onto a boat that was then towed into Sittwe's bay and sunk.

Mustak Ahmed managed to duck that initial round-up, which led to 1,000 arrests and hit the Rohingya with blunt force, but it was only really the beginning. The rest of his time in Sittwe was a dance with authorities hell-bent on taking Rohingya off the streets. "I had permission to go from Maungdaw to Sittwe, that's why I was not arrested. I had kept to their rules and regulations. They tried to arrest me a lot but I was under their law", he said. His mind was already obsessed about "rule and law" because he had always fastidiously paid attention to it and kept within the lines Myanmar set for the Rohingya, despite them constantly being redefined. They could not catch him on his permit so they found other questions to ask him. Had he informed the local administrator he was in town? Yes. He was, of course, operating squarely within the boundaries of "rule and law". His family, from a village where many were highly educated, had always taken diligent care of their papers. His father was a respected teacher and Mustak was himself studying to be a civil engineer.

The Sittwe arrests enraged some of those Rohingya who had held onto their arms from the Mujahideen days, and they decided to turn them against the government.[2] The response from the army was to crack down harder, adding outright violence to the repressive campaign of arrests that had already accompanied its so-called census. It also spread. Mustak had quickly retreated to Maungdaw for respite from the harassment, but Operation Nagamin followed him to the countryside. The steamers that had transported Rohingya through the region's river network were now a flotilla commandeered by the army, and wherever they docked uniforms streamed off and fanned out across northern Rakhine.

Mustak had some standing in the area and knew some of the military officers from university, and so he organised some chairs and a small reception customary for the visiting officials. His gesture was spurned. Past acquaintance was easily forgotten by those officials now focused on Ne Win's mission, and who immediately demanded that all villagers gather. The census began. Every villager was asked about their ancestry and how they could prove it. The officers produced an old map, written in a foreign language even Mustak could not identify, and asked the villagers to point to where they were from. Their arms were checked for scars, because according to a popular conspiracy theory vaccinations in East Pakistan and Myanmar were administered on opposing arms. A mark on the wrong side was indisputable proof that you were an illegal immigrant from Bangladesh.

"In our village, everyone was an original citizen of Myanmar. In Boli Bazar, there was no one from another country but there were some uneducated people who were arrested", said Mustak. "I saw that both in Sittwe and my village, people were harassed and people were oppressed. I saw it with my own eyes."

Mustak's father was also called.

"They found that there were certificates of my father who graduated in 1931, before independence, before the second world war. My father was more qualified than all of the officers there."

They stamped the back of his father's 1955 citizenship card: "certified".

* * *

Telegrams were arriving in Rangoon, addressed to its Rohingya residents and carrying warnings: do not return. The messages were sent by relatives already readying themselves to abandon Rakhine and unsure about what news had reached the capital. It was their last action before arriving on the Bangladeshi border, where a crisis was brewing and more telegrams were being sent—to London. Journalists were arriving alongside the Rohingya, eager to witness this major crisis of a new country, a Bangladesh born earlier that decade with a war that had forced its own population into refuge. Mustak had watched Operation Nagamin descend on Rakhine, flooding Sittwe with its deluge of uniforms, then spreading to northern Rakhine's countryside, where he witnessed his neighbours being questioned and then tied up and taken away. But the hysteria he was now hearing, the constant chatter of fear bubbling in Rohingya villages, made him wonder whether there was something he was not seeing, whether Nagamin was bearing a heavier toll elsewhere.

"When the operation began, all of the people were rushing to the border and trying to go to Bangladesh. There were people from ten villages near the border, along the Naf, who were leaving in particular. I hired a boat to go along the river and was surprised by what I saw. When I came to Zyongkhali village, there many people were coming. There was a big family and I asked them: why are you leaving? They said many people were arrested by the government so no one is staying here. I don't want to get arrested."

No one had asked Mustak to go but he felt a kind of responsibility after what he saw in his own village, where a lack of education and inability to communicate with the officers had damned some of his neighbours. The man he spoke to had not strayed far and invited Mustak to visit his home. To his surprise, they were the only people left in the village. Mustak believed that the Rohingya should have no reason to run. If only they would abide by rule and law, as most do, then the state would have no reason to expel them. The issue was making sure his people were aware of those rules and laws and adapted to the frequent changes designed to bureaucratically erase the Rohingya. After all, his own family had escaped trouble because his father had painstakingly documented their history. So, Mustak told the man not to join the people flooding into Bangladesh, to remain as the single family in this ghost village. He took the man to the Rakhine *ukatta* of another village and a permit was issued immediately. It was simple. Rule and law in operation.

But most did not have someone like Mustak to help them, who had studied with ethnic Rakhine and other ethnicities, people who were now officials and could communicate with them freely. Instead of a calming voice, they were surrounded by other fearful, hysterical Rohingya pushing towards the River Naf. Between March and July, around 200,000 Rohingya arrived in Bangladesh. They described soldiers turning up at villages, firing at young men and confiscating land. Women had been raped, they said, and though the numbers were unknown the news had reached every ear, fuelling the rush to Bangladesh.

"People fled because they saw others being arrested, they saw their property, their cattle, being taken away. That's why they feared being arrested themselves", said Mustak. "They didn't know why people were being arrested, they just saw that it was happening."

The Bangladesh they arrived in was one that had only won its independence from Pakistan seven years earlier. It was so poor it had been dismissed by the world as a country that could never develop. During the independence war in 1971, millions of

Bangladeshis became refugees in India while others had hidden in Burma, which Ne Win's authorities used to claim the whole Rohingya population was from Bangladesh. But it was now Bangladesh's turn to accept the refugees on its border. The Rohingya, who had lived in quiet, if imposed and uneasy, isolation, were now suddenly in the spotlight. The headlines that spoke of them for the first time initially struggled to understand who they were, tending to describe them as Arakan or Burmese Muslims before eventually naming them more specifically as Rohingya. An incoming humanitarian operation was asking how to handle them in a country so young. Bangladesh requested, and was granted, $15 million to set about creating the infrastructure for this new refugee population.

Within the first year, more than 12,000 died inside Bangladesh, far more than the likely number killed during Operation Nagamin itself. The majority of those deaths were avoidable. Bangladesh delivered the first of what would become eerily familiar statements proclaiming its generosity in sheltering the refugees. But by July 1978, only a few months after the refugees had begun arriving, Bangladesh had already signed a repatriation deal with Myanmar and set about creating the environment to implement it.

"Well, gentlemen, it is all very well to have fat, well-fed refugees", Syed Ali Khasru, then Secretary of the Ministry of Relief and Rehabilitation, told a meeting attended by UNHCR leaders. "But I must be a politician, and we are not going to make the refugees so comfortable that they won't go back to Burma."[3]

It would have been a struggle for any Rohingya to fatten themselves on the supplies they were given. In fact, when a UN nutritionist looked into whether the rations could sustain the population they found it was barely enough for basic survival, let alone to fuel the arduous daily tasks refugees had to carry out in search of water and fuel. The suggestion that Bangladesh could withhold food from the Rohingya should have shocked the UN leaders in the room. It was against the very principles of the 1951 refugee convention UNHCR based their work on, especially on the forced return of refugees "in any manner whatsoever". However, when the new UNHCR head for Cox's Bazar, Alan Lindquist, arrived in 1979 to investigate how the agency had behaved, he found something very different.

"None of the UN agency heads raised any objection to using food as a political weapon," Lindquist wrote in his 1979 review.[4]

Maung Kyaw Nu

Though the Rohingya had lived a relatively, but not wholly, untroubled life before 1978, they were also not equal in status to other ethnicities. They were not listed as indigenous to Burma but could get citizenship through other means, mostly by proving long ties to the country. So, when tens of thousands began to leave, Maung Kyaw Nu was worried the state would see this as a severing of those ties. The government was already claiming that the Rohingya flight simply proved the community was composed of interlopers from Bangladesh. That was why Mustak wanted the one family he found on the eastern banks of the River Naf to stay put in their village. The same thinking guided Maung Kyaw Nu when he met the refugees hiding in the forests of Maungdaw. He and a group of other students, whom Rohingya society afforded elevated status, met and voted to intercede on behalf of the terrified villagers. They decided they needed to convince them not to leave, provide them with food in the meantime and formulate a plan to send them home. But their promise did not hold. Maung Kyaw Nu, it turned out, was unable to deliver safety even for himself. His role in the 1974 student protests and that brief stint in jail had apparently marked his name as a potential troublemaker and he eventually heard news of a warrant for his arrest. He hid for a while, hoping he could ride out the threat, but realised the danger was real when a crumpled photocopy of the warrant against him was pressed into his hands.

A Rohingya rebel leadership of sorts already existed in Bangladesh, or "on the borders", as they described it. It was formed of students and elites like Maung Kyaw Nu who had already seen and experienced what he had. Some had left before Nagamin, turning in disgust from their home country after bad experiences like his on the boat; discriminated against at the checkpoints in Rakhine; or sensing the turn even earlier, after Ne Win took power. Maung Kyaw Nu slipped in amongst them, into a position of de-facto local leadership, mediating between the refugees and the Bangladeshi officials managing the crisis. They were fond of him, and government cars often rolled into the camps to ferry him to government offices for meetings about refugee demands or the increasing urgency from the Bangladeshi side to send them home. It was with a request for one of those meetings that he started the day he ended up in prison.

He waited, as usual, for the car to arrive at the entrance to the original Kutupalong camp, which had been established as one of the closest plots near Gundum, where many of the Rohingya had crossed over by land. Maung Kyaw Nu was received by the divisional commander, with whom he was friendly, and a number of soldiers. He expected to be taken to meet a foreign diplomat to whom he could pitch the Rohingya cause. Instead, they drove him straight to Chittagong and detained him. Bangladesh had more than tolerated the Rohingya rebel leadership up to that point, while it decided how to solve the crisis suddenly thrust upon it. That stance changed after it signed a repatriation agreement with Myanmar. Although he was given a good cell, usually reserved for VIPs, because of those relationships he had struck up with local officials, those same officials piled pressure on him when the meeting did eventually take place, inside the prison. "You better organise the people and send them back to Myanmar", a government official told him. He refused and stayed in prison another fifteen-and-a-half months.

As Bangladesh grew closer to Myanmar and its preferred option of repatriation, the relationship with the Rohingya leadership became increasingly disposable to the policymakers. They grew less concerned about the refugees' reactions to news of repatriation or the imprisonment of leaders like Maung Kyaw Nu. Bangladesh pushed on with its plans, and hostilities with the refugees increased—around 2,000 Rohingya were arrested. The government had eased its food cuts, which unsurprisingly led to a drop in the death rate. The same officer who had earlier met with UN leaders quickly renewed his threats to reduce food rations because of tensions over repatriation, claiming the issue of food had somehow, mysteriously to him, "gotten mixed up in politics". This time, UN agencies rejected the idea of restricting rations and made that clear to the government who, UNHCR's Lindquist suggested, realised the international criticism such a move would attract. So, on paper, it remained unchanged.

In the hands of the refugees, however, it was reduced. Food deliveries became irregular and occasionally rations were not provided at all. The government began to turn on the Bangladeshi Red Cross, accusing it of "spoiling" the refugees, threatening to close down its food programmes and ordering the arrests of some of its volunteers. It demanded UNHCR remove the head of their Cox's Bazar office. Bangladesh's bullishness on the issue and the deteriorating camp conditions eventually led to some international pressure where previously there had only been complicity. A report written by the US Embassy and then leaked to the press forced UNHCR to admit the true extent of the death rate. But Bangladesh also deemed its operation successful—the Rohingya were beginning to offer to return home. While 36,000 were returned by the end of the year, many of them after the food crisis, the rate increased to 25,000 a month on average in 1979. By March, according to the UN Human Rights Council, around half of the Rohingya had been returned.[5] Though UNHCR quietly criticised some of Bangladesh's policies, they were less vocal in public and played an active role in the repatriation. They also agreed to help Myanmar receive the refugees, assisting in the setting up of ten reception camps along the River Naf. The UN later repeatedly described the repatriation as voluntary, even after Lindquist accused Bangladesh of using food as a weapon.

"More surprising than the actions of the Bangladesh government toward the refugees, however, were those of the United Nations", wrote Lindquist, after wondering how Bangladesh had so quickly forgotten India's reception of Bangladeshi refugees in 1971. "Can there be any excuse for an international organisation like the United Nations High Commissioner for Refugees—whose brief is refugee welfare—to acquiesce in a policy which results in more than nine-thousand unnecessary deaths among a group of refugees? Certainly a UN agency is constrained by the policy of the country it is working in, but the UN's responsibility goes beyond that to any member government."[6]

UN reports in the aftermath and even into the 1990s frequently implied that, despite reporting rape and murder, the Rohingya had fled more out of fear of the army than actual widespread violence. A historical briefing even suggested the Rohingya were partially responsible for the violence that forced them away because they resisted the census process by resorting to "violent protests as well as acts of terrorism and sabotage". It also suggested much of the violence that did occur was caused by Rakhine neighbours, not the state.[7] In an editorial by *The Times*, which had covered the crisis through its reporter Richard Wigg, the Burmese explanation for the Rohingya exodus, which UNHCR seemed to have absorbed, was described as "disarmingly simple".[8]

THE ESCAPE VALVE

The briefing was written in 1995, by UNHCR's repatriation officer. A note at the end said his views did not necessarily represent those of the UN, but it was cited in UN documentation decades afterwards. By the time he was writing it, the UN were involved in another repatriation, of a larger number of Rohingya, who unquestionably had suffered at the hands of the state.

Mustak Ahmed

Inside a set of thin plastic wrappers, the type that seal at the top and usually contain *lungyis* or shirts sold from market stalls, Mustak Ahmed archives his dearest possessions—the precious family documents collected by his father and then himself. Shuffling through them takes him on a journey through the family history he kept alive, to a time before even his birth. The pride of his collection is a letter written in Burmese on a Victorian-era piece of parchment certified for postage with a stamp at the top for 8 annas (half a rupee). Hanging from the corner is the original, rusted paperclip. He also finds a copy of the certificate confirming his father's graduation as a teacher in 1932, then another from his completion of middle school twelve years earlier. Their packaging is humble, but the creased papers document more than a century of his family's life in Maungdaw.

He eventually finds the folded piece of blue card he has been looking for—his father's 1955 citizenship document. Glued to the front is a monochrome photo of his father wearing a beard and a tall cleric's hat and holding up his identity number. The card confirms the family's status as citizens of Burma and the purple stamp imprinted on it during Nagamin, more than twenty years after it was issued, confirms that status. With his palm resting on the sheets, Mustak reaffirms his catchphrase—"rule and law". The approval was marked on the card that day when the officers of Operation Nagamin came to Boli Bazar and found

Mustak's father more than ready to prove he belonged. A card issued to Mustak himself, only four years later, would cancel all of that out. His own card pointed out, very specifically, that it did not equal citizenship.

While Operation Nagamin tried to weed out the Rohingya without paperwork, the 1982 citizenship law introduced by Ne Win's government voided the documents of those who only years earlier had proved they belonged. Suddenly, all those records Mustak's family had kept meant very little. His family kept to Burma's rule and law only to see it changed to discard them. The citizenship law listed 135 ethnicities as native to Myanmar before British rule in 1824—but the Rohingya were excluded, essentially stripping the whole community of its citizenship in a single swoop. It was also a shift from the argument made only four years earlier, while in negotiations with Bangladesh, when Myanmar initially refused to accept Rohingya returnees: that the population were infiltrators who had arrived during and after Bangladesh's independence war with Pakistan.[9]

On 8 October 1982, Ne Win delivered a speech to promote the law. He spoke of Burma being able to shape its destiny, of "pure-blooded" citizens and "mixed blood" guests, and of drawing a line between Burma's history before and after British rule, when "foreigners, or aliens, entered our country un-hindered under various pretexts". Though his law effectively stripped citizenship from many minorities, and especially the Rohingya, Ne Win presented it all as an opportunity for those without status "to escape from a life of uncertainty" that could offer opportunity for future generations "if they live correctly and properly". They would be given "the right to earn according to their work and live a decent life. No more." In the meantime, however, not being a citizen had consequences that involved exclusion from public life.

"We will have to leave them out in matters involving the affairs of the country and the destiny of the State", said Ne Win. "This is not because we hate them. If we were to allow them to get into positions where they can decide the destiny of the State and if they were to betray us we would be in trouble."[10]

Though being excluded from the indigenous races of Burma stripped Rohingya of full citizenship, the 1982 law technically provided some pathways towards a sort of second-class "associate citizenship". It was still hard to obtain, setting high barriers for the applicant like proof of pre-1948 citizenship in their family and being able to speak an indigenous language. For many of the Rohingya, deprived of education in neglected Rakhine, this was beyond their means. But Mustak had everything he needed.

Alongside his trove of documents is an A4-sized notebook he guards jealously. Though faded by time, its hardbound cover has protected the pages inside through several decades and from the humidity that often condemns fragile textiles to mould. Every now and again he takes a break from talking to spend a few moments flicking through its pages, looking for something specific until, eventually, he finds it. In this case, it is a handwritten table listing his family members, their dates of birth and a serial number. The string of digits corresponds to the applications he made for citizenship in 1989, an attempt to regain it after several years of being officially considered a "resident foreigner", written down in the presence of the immigration officer handling the application. He took home and kept hold of a copy of the filled-in form and its evidence of the family's roots. All of this information and all of the paperwork he submitted as evidence should have met those demands required for the second-class citizenship he sought. The application was never rejected, but citizenship never came.

"All of our documents are with the immigration department. They know the truth."

* * *

The Rohingya very much believe in the truth of their ties to the land of Rakhine. They speak of it without any grand posturing or rhetoric around what belongs to them or others. They speak only of their connection to their "Golden Arakan" and that they remember no other home. This truth is largely unwritten and that makes it hard to prove and easy to deny. When the military government claimed the Rohingya snuck in pretending to be refugees in 1971, families with centuries of history, through to the pre-Bamar Arakan Kingdom, had no way of proving it. But Mustak was very aware that these documents he holds dear are the written form of the basic Rohingya truth. He could brandish them in response to the lies he says the government tells about the Rohingya. Where other Rohingya struggle to even communicate with the authorities, let alone prove their right to live in the places they were born, Mustak speaks freely in Burmese. Unlike most, he has the staggeringly unusual privilege of being able to cite his exact age because he demanded government offices hand over birth certificates. Mustak occupied a reality in Rakhine where the government was not totally absent. In fact, their presence allowed the family to go to unusual lengths to archive their history, proven only through their interactions with that state—in birth, through education, or in death.

He clung to the documents, but in reality they meant little to Myanmar. But his was not the only family who had at least some sort of record of their existence. The dirt around homes in northern Rakhine has often been turned by instruments digging a safe place to secure those documents by Rohingya preparing to run, scared they might lose them during the escape to storms or the Naf's waters and hoping the papers would survive the coming fires. They were often not, however, able to return to excavate their evidence because the violence that raged through Rakhine did not stop to ask for citizenship.

If Nagamin signalled the start of a Rohingya consciousness about the existential threat facing the community, then the 1982 law was the moment that threat was confirmed. It not only altered their legal status but also marked a real and permanent change that would evolve over time, punctuated by violent rifts, into the reality that by 2018 would finally be described as genocide. Whether individual Rohingya could be citizens or not was not important; the whole community was now classified as foreign. Though the move was branded as a way to deliver justice for the "pure blooded" against colonial encroachment, it was the British-era Registration of Foreigners Law that could now be used to codify restrictions on Rohingya movement, that demanded they had permits to move beyond their own townships. To stay overnight in another village required another permit from the local headman. Access to education was increasingly stripped away and familiarity with violence became more usual.

The 1988 pro-democracy protests provided another jolt to the military regime that would eventually be felt by the Rohingya, some of whom participated in the nationwide protests but had no distinctive role in the movement. It initially appeared to have forced Ne Win from power when he made a show of stepping down as party chairman. Warning the protesters in his farewell speech, he declared that "when the Army shoots, it shoots to hit".[11] A coup that put the army back in control, thought to have been orchestrated by Ne Win himself, was completed by September 1988, only a few months after his supposed departure. It now ruled after having faced down its most serious threat from a tired population. Its wrath then appeared to turn, once again, to the frontier regions—Rakhine State among them. The Rohingya had been systematically stripped of rights since the 1982 citizenship law, but its combination with the new military reality after the 1988 movement was devastating. There were increasing numbers of military deployments to Rakhine, alongside other parts of the country, as the junta set out to remind a rebellious population of the pressure its grip could exert.

"If I wanted to go to Maungdaw, it wasn't possible," said Mustak. "If I wanted to go to Buthidaung, it wasn't possible. They restricted our travel and to go anywhere, we needed permission. Before, we used to write on our documents 'Rohingya' but they didn't do that anymore. They started calling us Bengali."

The military had been resettling populations into towns it controlled around Myanmar, and by 1989 this campaign reached Sittwe. Rakhine communities were shifted into Rohingya villages, which felt put out and were often displaced by the new reality.[12] Soldiers quickly followed and a trend of militarisation continued into the 1990s that, by its very nature, required a massive amount of labour—labour that was found among the Rohingya. A UN special rapporteur sent in 1993 reported that thousands of porters drafted around the country since 1988 had been killed, naming "Myanmar Muslims of Rakhine State" first in a list of the most affected groups. Myanmar did not deny that its forces relied on the labour of the population, but reframed it as a contribution from the people towards the nation.

"[O]ur religion [Buddhism] taught us that these deeds are the noblest of all and merit attained from them will surely lead to a longer life leading to the attainment of Nibbana, which is the liberation of both mind and body from all forms of attachment", a government statement said of the forced portering. "If some people think that contributing labour is the same as 'slave labour' that has been forced upon the people", the statement went on, casting aspersions on those who complained, implying they were foreign, "then we must say that they have a lot to learn about our traditions, our culture and way of life here."[13]

By 1991, the boats on the Naf once again found themselves shuttling urgently between its banks loaded with humans, instead of floating along its length in search of fish. The stories its passengers carried in lieu of belongings were of the uniforms now everywhere and the men who had disappeared. This time the operation was called Pyi Thaya (Operation Clean and Beautiful Nation). Many of the arrivals were women who had decided to take their children to safety, unsure whether or not their husbands would return from forced labour. Others came with their husbands immediately after they returned, drained, ill and with a resolve to never again work in those jungles. The UN asked 500 families about why they came. Almost half of them said their wives had been raped by soldiers.

Shob Mehraj

Shob Mehraj's husband left for the jungle as one of thirty men. He was assigned when soldiers marched over from their barracks and demanded the village's regular quota of workers from the village chairman. So, he patrolled the village, occasionally dangling his finger over crowds of men and settling on certain individuals who were then pulled from the crowd and gathered by the soldiers, ready to be marched away. Only six of them returned. Those few who did come back were infuriated about being sent. They argued with the village committee, whose only response was that the order had come from higher up. They too either complied or died.

The porters were called "coolies" by the military, echoing the colonial-era term given to low-caste labourers in British India, and were forced to walk ahead of the soldiers, acting as human shields as the army ventured into the thick jungle. The army claimed Operation Pyi Thaya was about flushing out the fighters of the Rohingya Solidarity Organisation (RSO), which had been founded after the community was stripped of its citizenship in a bid to fight for the return of those rights. Even by the early 1990s, when forced labour was at its height, RSO had carried out very few operations against the Burmese military, but maintained a presence in the jungles where they trained. Some estimates suggested Rohingya militias collectively held only 150 fighters by 1994.[14] No Rohingya saw any soldier die under any kind of RSO attack. Occasionally, they heard gunfire from somewhere ahead of them, and when the soldiers reappeared without their Rohingya labourers they claimed there had been a gunfight.

The rest of the job involved carrying heavy loads along jungle tracks already trampled by the bare feet of other Rohingya porters before them. They were watched by soldiers always prepared to punish whoever struggled to carry the army's baggage along these craggy paths. Sometimes, once they had reached the top of an incline, a soldier would kick a tired porter downhill and leave him for dead. For periods of fifteen days or more, they lived in servitude, without time to eat or bathe or pray. When they returned, they watched the village chairman walking up to the next set of men, pointing them out from the crowd and declaring their time to meet the army's requested quota had come. They knew some of these men would not return and those who did would not be spared for long before having to repeat the task.

For a year before Shob Mehraj's husband was taken for labour, the situation had been getting worse. The government she had never known as a child was now everywhere. The timing, some had suggested, was the result of the military seeking a distraction from growing national unrest over its decision to discard a 1990 election won by Aung San Suu Kyi—an election in which the Rohingya had been allowed to vote. Shortly afterwards, there was an influx of soldiers into Rakhine, followed by more violence against Rohingya.

"There was no safety for us, even in our own houses", Shob Mehraj recalls. When the men were taken, the soldiers "would come in and torture the women". When they left it was only temporary. They returned, in different bodies but the same uniforms, for more torture, a morbid promise delivered each time alongside a demand: leave. "Where would we go?" she asked them. They said: "Wherever you want." Then the uniforms strolled over to their plots of land, eyed them, pressed the soil under their military boots, then measured it and jotted down a note. They declared the land seized. It belonged to the state. The state that had no desire for the people sitting on the land to remain.

Not long after Shob Mehraj's husband returned, the family decided they could no longer stay in the village, so they decided to go to Sittwe. The army was everywhere along the route, stopping the family and asking whether they were going to Bangladesh. Though that possibility was very real in her mind, she denied it and told them the family were taking their child for vaccinations at the hospital in Sittwe. She stayed with her sister when she arrived, but it was immediately obvious that Operation Pyi Thaya had not spared Sittwe either. Fires and arrests spread everywhere and so they decided not to risk staying still while there were tens of thousands already heading to Bangladesh.

Her family settled in Gundum. Other families settled in places like it. They were places on the borders, with names assigned to fields and scatterings of homesteads rather than recognisable villages. They became the camps remembered only by those who stayed there, soon forgotten when they were dismantled, their residents sent home soon after arrival or funnelled a little further inland, where Kutupalong and Nayapara refugee camps were born and lasted far longer than anyone imagined.

4

THE ARRIVAL

Momtaz (September 2017)

Cyclone Mora arrived in the June before the Tatmadaw swept a new set of Rohingya into Bangladesh in numbers larger than ever before. It did what cyclones do and what Bangladesh is accustomed to, but the country's storm shelters had been built with only the local villages in mind—they had no space for the refugees. There was nowhere to turn to for shelter when the 150km winds tore roofs off Rohingya houses and split their bamboo skeletons, destroying a quarter of their homes regardless of whether people were registered as refugees or not. The plastic cards issued by the UN granted no safety from the cyclone.

Bangladesh's cyclone season makes way for the monsoon through August and into September, only to return shortly afterwards for a second spell of heavy winds that add new bite to the wetness that still lingers. This was what Momtaz was stepping into, with nothing. Heavy gusts and rain swirled overhead, unfiltered by the trees that should have provided protection but had been scythed down to house the refugees and supply the fuel needed for cooking. They had started out living on the sides of the road, only metres from where they had been hauled from the river or swampy fields by locals who had seen the fires from their own homes and soldiers who ignored orders not to intervene. Individual tragedies were piled on to the collective during those chaotic days—cars rushing past on Teknaf Road's single-lane highway frequently mowed down stray refugees. In the forests, confused elephants trampled tents and some of the people inside them. After a few weeks, having muddled through its attempt to mount a response far larger than anticipated, Bangladesh realised that what was happening was nothing like the past. It asked the Rohingya sat on the roadside and in the forest to move further inland, directing them towards the forested hills south of Kutupalong and giving birth to its newest annex, "Balukhali-2".

This new reality was taking shape by the time Momtaz emerged from the hospital. Her face was still encased in a tangle of bandages that hid all but her right ear, left eye and mouth. She stepped into the sludge of the camp with nothing, as if she had just arrived from Myanmar, her limited vision filled with this apocalyptic sight. Clasping Rozeya's hand, she settled on her haunches on the edge of this nascent settlement and waited for someone to help her find her place in it. Whoever had carried the unconscious pair to safety and taken them to hospital was now gone and everything familiar had been stripped from her, apart from the small head she clutched to her chest, shorn of hair by the doctors who had stitched Rozeya's wounds back together. No one in Kutupalong had much, but Momtaz had even less and so she begged—for something to eat, or for somewhere to stay, or simply for some advice on where she could hide from the menacing clouds above. Though those who trundled past under the weight of bamboo poles and heavy sacks had little themselves, they did help. Though not a single person felt any *shanti*, the sight of Momtaz was somehow worse. She was given the simple materials to strap together a shelter, and people volunteered to help her do it.

When she spoke to the people around and they heard Tula Toli's name mentioned through the muffle of her bandages, people knew where to find her old neighbours. The village was already known for its horrors. A helper guided Momtaz to Balukhali-2 and the new Tula Toli nestled inside it. The village no longer existed in its traditional sense, but instead had become a community of a few hundred exiled survivors living in their little corner where no physical boundary separated them from the rest of Kutupalong, just the knowledge that these were the tents where nightmares were felt most vividly in a place where sleep troubled a million people most nights. It was Momtaz's aunt who first heard that a Tula Toli survivor had arrived: "People were terrified when they saw her approach. She looked like a dead body, covered in white bandages."

Living with the aunt was Momtaz's youngest sister, who resembled Momtaz in a more innocent state. Tayyiba had lived up on a hill in Tula Toli, above the carnage, with a vantage point that enabled her to see what was happening below and a distance that let her escape. She thought none had survived, just as Momtaz had assumed. Tayyiba had fled to the forests, wracked by the certainty that her sisters were dead but with her own family intact, her husband and children still with her. It was the sisters' aunt who had dragged Tayyiba to safety and then taken on the family's mothering role, always sitting in the background offering support, advice and filling in the silences when her nieces' throats sealed against their words. Tayyiba asked about the other sisters and their mother and fed her eldest sister all she had, although Momtaz could not eat much. In their new Tula Toli, Momtaz found a way to settle. She built a new shelter on the first increment of the same incline as Tayyiba's, directly above the new dirt path that doubled as a road into a newly forming market run for the refugees. The most ordinary of rain showers drummed a heavy rhythm on the tarpaulin canopy of her new home, the sound filling the tiny room that still felt empty in all the space unfilled by missing family members. Momtaz and Rozeya clutched each other.

One day, when the rain was still coming down on their heads and the floor outside still swept the tired feet from underneath the refugees, there came word of a ghost. A man approached Momtaz in the street. He spoke of another woman who also came from Tula Toli, with similar scars and a face like Momtaz's, and who was living in another camp. She had just come out of hospital, her arms gripping a girl who looked a little like Rozeya, but taller, and whose hair was also cropped to reveal a crude scar running across the crown of her head. No husband or parent surrounded them, no brother or sister pressed up against the girl's shoulder. But this image was a cracked reflection of Momtaz, an image that would have to remain living only in her head, beyond her reach. The man had no information about where this ghost of Tula Toli had wandered next and, though Momtaz asked in alleyways, she still had little strength. She believed the man, but it could have been anyone. Tula Toli had left behind many widows and orphans.

Dildar came back to life at a funeral. As Momtaz crouched on her heels outside a tent where sullen-faced mourners sniffled and whispered prayers, she learned from another that she could end her own mourning for her younger sister. She had not only been seen but identified by an old neighbour, living somewhere on the other side of the hills south of Balukhali. This confirmation put new strength into Momtaz's recovering legs, and she started to search for Dildar in Thaingkali camp. Now she had narrowed down the area in which her younger sister was staying, it did not take long to find her.

I first met Momtaz not long afterwards. Though I did not realise it at first, Dildar was sitting in the shadows, filling the gaps in Momtaz's story. My translator, Yassin, a Rohingya who lives near the Tula Toli enclave, did not realise it either. When he had last spoken to Momtaz, he thought she was her family's only survivor. Dildar was echoing Momtaz's experience, able to describe the insides of the homes as the fires raged, and the actions of the soldiers, not because she had heard the stories recounted by her sister but because her final day in Tula Toli had been identical.

As Momtaz slowly pieced her family and life back together, the refugees were still coming. The numbers were lower, but still victims of military violence fled an operation that had not yet shed its last blood. The stragglers were also coming, whose villages had been spared but who were terrified by the sound and smell of death that hung like a fog over northern Rakhine. On their arrival, they would have noticed the banners strung up everywhere they turned, hung by officials or village politicians seeking favour with the ruling Awami League party. They declared Prime Minister Sheikh Hasina the "Mother of Humanity". With some international nudging, Hasina had been persuaded to leave the borders open and Bangladesh wanted everyone to know it was ready, this time, to be a champion of the Rohingya. The aid community was given full access for the first time and the army was deployed to organise the camps and pacify any local agitators, including the criminals who had already started making money off the backs of the unfortunate. Bangladeshi ministers released themselves from previous restraint to lambast their eastern neighbours, while plans to launch an International Criminal Court case against Myanmar were announced. Locals who had detested the Rohingya were suddenly on board, many struck with sympathy and others enticed by the employment they anticipated arriving with the aid workers. Whatever their motivation, there was more goodwill than ever before.

But the families arriving did not easily find their relatives who already lived in Bangladesh. They were processed in the transit camp near Kutupalong and then rested for a few days. Their health was checked and they were registered. Some sacks of rations and a bucket were handed over to help them start their new lives. However, the government had already started to alter its course. If there were going to be a million refugees, they would not be allowed to do anything more than be refugees. Phones were banned (for security reasons according to the government, although it also successfully made life more uncomfortable for the Rohingya) and that meant when sisters like Momtaz and Dildar needed to find each other, it was going to be by foot.

Their reunion was difficult. Each had settled in different parts of the camp superstructure, under different *majhis* (Rohingya contacts in the camps for government authorities, each one responsible for 100 families), and moving closer to each other could risk losing their access to aid. They had no way of communicating, so spending time together involved hoping the other was home after clambering over a hill and through some fields, or if there was some spare change by way of a donation, taking the electric buggies that plied Teknaf Road, shuttling between the camps. But there was value in it. Though Tayyiba was around, and much closer to Momtaz's home, she had a family around her. When Momtaz and Dildar were together, the empty spaces in their shelters filled out a little. Their relationship was not perfect. Sometimes their personalities grated. Momtaz was vivacious and a bit erratic, sometimes, for the sensibilities of the more straight-laced Dildar. The company they gave each other had warmth, but was not exuberant or playful. It lay in the tears they shed for each other, angry that a sister experienced what they had themselves, and in supportive smiles and the time spent together, stroking a niece's cropped hair as the rain hammered away only a few inches overhead.

Anwara Begum

Anwara Begum was still only a teen, but by 1991 she was married, a parent, and already one among crowds crossing into

Bangladesh, for the second time in her life. Like Shob Mehraj, her husband Ruhul Amin had been taken as a "coolie" for the military and returned with the same resolve to go to Bangladesh before he could be drafted again. As it would when she returned in 2017, the monsoon season loomed overhead. If she could not remember her first refuge, then the second was unforgettably haunted by the wetness that ate into the bamboo and soaked the ground she sat upon. The winds howled with threats the family's bamboo shelter could not hold against, so they pulled the tarpaulin from the roof and huddled together with the sheet wrapped tightly around them. Even the fires they crouched around while boiling a pot of rice spread an acrid spoke fed by the moisture in their firewood. It filled the chest. Her child developed a cough. For two weeks, she spent every day trudging the miserable path uphill, through sodden earth her feet sank into with each step, to find a clinic for her child strapped to her back. But there were few hospitals and the NGO clinics had no access to effective medicine. She was given paracetamol. After several days, the baby's cough had not improved but it was also getting no worse. His chest heaved and he didn't sleep well, but it went no further. Then one night, he did not wake.

Anwara had already lost her first child days after its birth in Myanmar. Now her second child had died, away from the home she had tried to save him from. Death existed in both places. It had to be dodged in Myanmar, but there was something inevitable about an early end to life in Bangladesh—where death hung over their heads like a tarpaulin that offered no shelter, casting a shadow that offered no coolness from the heat but bitter cold when it was least wanted.

The stories of violence that were carried across the River Naf were stopped by neither monsoon nor cyclone. Women kept arriving with children but without husbands. They were not returning from porter duty. Some were presumed dead and others were confirmed so by returning neighbours—shot because they had fallen ill while hauling a soldier's load through the jungle and for becoming a burden. Others were shot in more mysterious circumstances. The Rohingya fighters that Myanmar was supposedly targeting had still not launched any kind of insurgency. Nurul Islam, a law graduate who had studied in Yangon became an RSO leader after humiliations at Rakhine checkpoints convinced him of the state's institutionalised racism. According to him, disagreements over strategy were a constant cause of fractures that meant the RSO never moved beyond planning. In the meantime, Myanmar turned its crosshairs on Bangladesh as well, accusing it of backing the rebels and turning a blind eye to weapons smuggling. Myanmar stationed its troops on the border and pointed China-supplied heavy artillery westwards. But not long after the refugees arrived, Bangladesh was ready to abandon them again. By November 1991, the border stand-off ended and the government signed agreements with Myanmar.

Death lingered on both sides of the River Naf, and Anwara's family had to decide on which bank they would resign themselves to. Despite their loss, Anwara and her husband Nur Alam tried at first to avoid returning to Myanmar. His experience of forced labour and the violence they saw on the journey was enough to permanently fear it. But life was also getting worse in Bangladesh as the government continued to force the refugees back across the border. They eventually caved in. It was there, on that boat heading across the Naf, that Anwara made the oath never to return. It was the same oath she broke more than twenty years later when she saw the bodies floating down from Tula Toli.

* * *

Bangladesh's first repatriation in 1978 had provided the government a blueprint for handling the Rohingya. Not long after their arrival, it had again signed an agreement with Myanmar for their return and there was little in the way of hand-wringing over its implementation. Food rations were reduced, community leaders were jailed and squads of uniformed officers beat refugees. In some cases, forms were handed over to refugees, though observers said the Rohingya felt obliged to agree and that some of them simply did not understand what they were signing because it was in English. In one case, interviews by UNHCR turned up 332 people who said they did not want to return, but by the next day Bangladesh told UNHCR that half of them had suddenly changed their minds. UNHCR suspected coercion. Consent forms, forcibly signed or not, were not always necessary. Humanitarian access to the camps was restricted and soldiers began to turn up at night with a simple order for families to pack up. Bangladesh was not their home and their real homes were now safe, so it was time to return, the soldiers said. Some knew families who had already returned and thought maybe the soldiers were telling the truth. Others had seen fights break out between refugees and security forces. So, when the uniforms came, they listened and boarded the buses that had come to take them to the river.

All of these signs initially prompted UNHCR to warn against a repetition of the policies that had killed so many in the 1978 repatriations. In 1992, it withdrew from the process but only a year later resumed its cooperation, insisting that Bangladesh had stopped its use of coercion. By 1994, UNHCR were actively encouraging Rohingya to return and even claimed 95 per cent of refugees had opted for repatriation.[1] To prove it, they invited an American researcher who was writing a report about the process for the US Congress. Their plan backfired. The researcher witnessed everyone bursting into tears when they were told where the boats were going.

Families were rounded up and held in a camp next to the Naf. The camp was called "Rohingyakhali". When the monsoon was heavy, they could be held there for a fortnight as they waited, repeating the nervous transit they had found on arrival in Bangladesh. Women whose husbands were in jail were shipped back to the camps. The rest were loaded onto the coastguard's motor boats, deployed to maximise their efficiency in spiriting refugees out of Bangladesh. Instead of individual interviews, UNHCR had used mass registrations that assumed refugees wanted to return unless they voiced an objection. MSF did their own survey and found that, in stark contrast to UNHCR's claim that the entire refugee population wanted to return, almost two-thirds said they did not want to return but a similar amount were not even aware that they could refuse.

The conditions that UNHCR had adjudged to be safe were unclear. They had only themselves been given access to Rakhine four months earlier and though Myanmar had agreed to take the refugees back, after massive international criticism and diplo-matic talks with Bangladesh, the Rohingya were still not viewed as citizens. There was relative calm, but certainly no peace and no promise of lasting safety. Foreign minister U Ohn Gyaw made that clear in 1992 when he reiterated the fact that the Rohingya had not been listed among Myanmar's "national races":

"Historically, there has never been a 'Rohingya' race in Myanmar", he said. "Since the First Anglo-Myanmar War in 1824, people of Muslim faith from the adjacent country illegally entered Myanmar Naing-Ngan, particularly Rakhine State. Being illegal immigrants, they do not hold any immigration papers like the other nationals of the country. In the present case, the num-ber of people who dare not submit themselves to the routine scrutiny of national registration cards by immigration officials fled to the neighbouring country. It is not a unique experience for such occurrences regularly took place when immigration checks are executed. It should be categorically stated that there is no persecution whatever based on religious ground."[2]

In 1978, the UN had overlooked Rohingya reluctance to return. They had not even asked whether they had been forced to leave or if the food shortages had played a part in their returns. When 9,000 refugees ripped up any papers they had from Myanmar, hoping it would mean they would not be processed on their return, the UN did not bat an eyelid. But this was later seen as a failure of the lack of procedure at the time. By 1991, the UN had developed policies specifically around ensuring repatriations were voluntary. There were lessons they should have learned, especially the stripping of Rohingya citizenship only four years after it was deemed they could safely return to Myanmar.

But the UN's failures were documented twenty years later, in an internal document they have never released because it was so damning. It recognised that, during the two repatriations, UNHCR had arguably "departed the furthest from its protection mandate and principles in any of its operations worldwide." In its opening passages, it posed a question even more relevant now: why had the number of Rohingya in Bangladesh not decreased over the decades despite those repatriations? They may not have imagined that seven years later the population would be far larger. The report said, "at a minimum, UNHCR showed reckless disregard for its protection mandate", citing the body's knowledge of fifteen refugees killed and 900 imprisoned for protests that were put down by the Bangladeshi authorities. They knew a child had been arrested when he was tasked with delivering a letter, objecting to the repatriations, to a visiting UNHCR official because the men who wrote it thought that would be a safer option than speaking out. But they and the whole humanitarian system decided not to go public with their concerns about repatriation and tried to deal with the issue through back channels. It was here that the discussions stayed, in offices between UN officials and the government, while the Rohingya themselves were given no stake. Unsurprisingly, most Rohingya began to believe they could not say no to the government or UNHCR, and so their doubts were not recorded in UNHCR registration drives which considered refugees willing to be repatriated unless they said otherwise. This suited Geneva, who wanted their local staff to push ahead with the process. At one meeting at headquarters, its approach to Rohingya voices was made clear by a senior official: "The Rohingyas are primitive people. At the end of the day, they will go where they are told to go."

5

THE LONG HAUL

The 1990s

Kutupalong and Nayapara are twins of an unplanned birth. They are encampments but they also breathe, expanding as refugees rush in and contracting whenever Bangladesh expels them with sudden, determined exhalation. They are the twins Bangladesh has never wanted and has never ceased trying to be rid of. They have remained, and have been forgotten, neglected and rejected by all others. Though Bangladesh has tried to sweep them away from its southeastern hills, the camps have refused to disappear, their roots instead tunnelling deeper into the dusty land they were pitched upon—simultaneously becoming a part of their environment, both natural and human, and at odds with it.

They were initially among twenty-two settlements that absorbed the 250,000 Rohingya who fled to Bangladesh from 1991 onwards. But as others were emptied by Bangladesh's repatriation campaigns, allowing the paddy fields and forest to return, the residents left behind were pushed towards the larger settlements that morphed into what would officially become the only two remaining refugee camps. Locals bemoaned the Rohingya presence and called them criminals, but grew used to them, turning to them for their own needs. The entrepreneurs of Cox's Bazar found business supplying the camps. Landowners drew from them cheap labour for the fields around Kutupalong or to harvest the salt produced by pumping the Naf's salty water into barren fields near Nayapara and leaving it to evaporate. The exploitative sought out uneducated and unemployed youth, the cogs for the types of illicit businesses common to any border.

By the mid-1990s, Bangladesh had once again forced many of the Rohingya back to Myanmar but, unlike the aftermath of Operation Nagamin, was unable to complete the process within a year—let alone meet the six-month target set out in its deal with Myanmar. Bangladesh's threats, forced hunger and empty guarantees of safety were familiar, but in Myanmar much had changed. If many of the Rohingya who had fled in 1978 had simply feared violence and arrest, rather than having experienced it first-hand as many in positions of authority implied, then the decade since had acquainted them well with the military's force. Though the majority were repatriated by 1995, when UNHCR fully participated, the process stretched on in fits and starts through the decade, with more arriving as others left and tens of thousands, registered under UNHCR before Bangladesh stopped officially acknowledging refugees in 1992, refusing to budge.

This frustrated the government, especially after Myanmar also decided to become more difficult and refused to take back the majority of the remaining refugees. Months became years and still the refugees remained. Bangladesh's annoyance began to boil over. In April 1996, fifteen young women and children who were arriving in Bangladesh were pushed back out and drowned while being towed across the Naf. Then, in 1997, authorities took the level of coercion to a new level and seized 399 refugees from Kutupalong and Nayapara and forced them back to Myanmar at gunpoint. Outrage at this blatant breach of the principles of non-refoulement, even for a country that did not recognise the 1951 Refugee Convention, brought a momentary end to repatriation. By this point, Kutupalong and Nayapara still held more than 20,000 registered refugees—though the figure was never reflective of the true number of Rohingya living in Bangladesh. Because the country had refused to register refugees since 1992, instead declaring them illegal immigrants, those that arrived afterwards were uncounted. Banned from living in the actual refugee camps, they settled amongst the local population or in makeshift settlements that had spilled out of Kutupalong and Nayapara.

* * *

The freshness of their trauma did not convince Bangladesh of the need to change tack, and as long as the refugees were arriving in uneven scatterings it would not be forced to confront the problem. The global gaze rarely turned to Bangladesh apart from in times of catastrophic flooding. The country had no intention of supporting the new refugees in Kutupalong or Nayapara, which it hoped would soon be gone altogether. Its plan was to have a country clear of Rohingya and if the refugees would not return— even through a system rigged to ensure they barely understood what they were consenting to, if they consented at all— Bangladesh would make the refugees very aware of the government's intentions. The environment went from difficult to outright hostile. Bangladeshi officers harassed Rohingya outside their homes and often empowered locals to participate. The ration reductions that killed more than 10,000 in 1978 to encourage the refugee population's return were repurposed into a policy more targeted, more specifically punitive: families who actively refused repatriation were punished by having their ration books withdrawn.

Zia and Nobi

To Ziaur Rahman, it felt like torture—as though his family were being punished for their persecution, while no one came to investigate and even UN workers turned a blind eye. A child of the camps, he had landed in Bangladesh only a few years after his birth, an age so young he remembered almost nothing of Myanmar. But it was children like "Zia" that the government seemed so agitated about. If they did not return, the thinking went, those children would assimilate into Bangladesh society. Of even greater concern were the ones only a few years younger than Zia, born inside the refugee camps, who might even try to apply for citizenship under the confused laws that potentially granted nationality to anyone born within the country's boundaries. Zia's family refused to return to Myanmar, but had no aspirations to become Bangladeshi. Their refusal was based solely on the fear of what they faced on their return—and they were punished for it. Their ration book was confiscated and Zia's uncle imprisoned on trumped-up charges. The family were told the condition of his release was their signature on the repatriation form.

"My uncle was one time [in prison for] five years, another time seven years", said Zia. "Not only my uncle, many Rohingya, they had to go to the court to appear. In one month [maybe he has to appear] two times. One Rohingya has three cases, one Rohingya has four cases, five. Why does this happen? Because they were refusing to go back to Myanmar. So you cannot be a good person in society. If the community chose you as leader or selects you as a good person, then the government will arrest you or kill you."

Zia grew up in Nayapara, a childhood friend and classmate of Nobi's, but his family were regularly shifted about. His mother had been separated from her own parents and siblings and was not allowed to settle in one place. The uncertainty was supposed to force them to accept their fate in Myanmar. Instead, they went on hunger strike, as did dozens of families in response to the forced repatriation of 1997. Some even tried to free the detained refugees, who were locked up overnight, by attacking the police station with bows and arrows and iron clubs. Bangladesh's enforced uncertainty could not override their fears of returning, renewed each time a new family arrived with confirmation that Rakhine still offered no peace.

With them were tens of thousands of children whom Bangladesh did not want to go to school, certainly not beyond the most primary of levels. It considered education a potential stay factor, like the food that might create the "well-fed" refugees they were so keen to avoid in 1978. It was also concerned about young Rohingya assimilation. Bangladesh insisted that it had only ever accepted the Rohingya out of choice, not duty, but had no plan to integrate them. The plan went beyond neglect. When it came to educating the Rohingya, the authorities actively sabotaged any attempt to build a self-sufficient generation within the camps.

* * *

When the UN promotes its work in refugee camps, it is usually with pictures of beaming children standing in front of the blue-and-white logos of its various agencies and carrying the blue backpacks handed out to them. Nobi did not own one of those bags to carry his books in—though nothing would have been as precious to him. His study materials instead lived underneath bedding, hidden away. They were read beneath the blankets he crouched under during the night, one hand holding down the pages and the other balancing a kerosene lamp, like a rebellious child staying up after bedtime. He trained his ears to listen beyond the fabric barrier around his head, for the sound of heavy rubber soles in the darkness outside, crunching on the dust in the dry months and squidging in the mush after it had rained. Neither he nor his parents wanted to explain to a patrolling soldier why he was studying.

Their shelter was typical for a Rohingya family in Bangladesh. It was without adornments and filled only with whatever helped them survive. Nobi owned little other than a lifetime of experiences gathered living in Bangladesh, as a child in the 1990s and a teen in the 2000s. They had taught him that he was a refugee. That was his identity, at least in the eyes of those people who used his status in life to hold power over him but never to give him rights. A refugee, he had also learned, was not allowed to study. This preyed on the minds of Rohingya parents, who feared a "lost generation" deprived of hope and forced into delinquency or worse. It also preyed on the minds of those who had been able to study in Myanmar's university system, before everything about their lives had unravelled. If Bangladesh would not provide schooling beyond the most basic of levels, then, the teachers resolved, they would do it themselves. Many already taught in the basic primary schools run by the UN, but started to sandwich those shifts between private classes in the early mornings and late at night, held within their own shelters or later in separate classrooms made with the same materials. They charged nominal costs that simply allowed the schools to operate. Instead of the basic nursery-rhyme rote learning of UN schools, they taught Burmese, English and whatever else was needed to pass exams that could allow them to go into higher education if that possibility was ever opened to them.

Nobi's brother pulled him from the religious schools he had been studying in, the only types Bangladesh really allowed the Rohingya to operate with relative freedom, and put him into one of these schools. Here, he became classmates with Zia, his neighbour in Nayapara. The two studied English and Maths and a shifting set of other topics their teachers dared to teach, while bypassing Bangladeshi history in order to avoid being accused of trying to assimilate. The friends quickly rose to the top of their classes, and not long afterwards were assigned to tutor pupils only a couple of years their junior. Their families cobbled together the money that brokers demanded to arrange Bangladeshi ID cards—enough to let them sit the national exams, even if they might not be able to do anything with them afterwards. The boys spent marathon cramming sessions locked together inside their bamboo schools.

They were a pair of skinny young boys enthused by their educational achievements and determined to use them. They dressed like teachers, in shirts tucked into trousers, wore smart, perfectly combed haircuts and were always clean-shaven. They walked confidently through the alleyways of Nayapara, not from arrogance but because education bestowed upon them a respect that transcended age. They had purpose and it was clear to everyone. But success quickly exposed them to the security apparatus that encircled and infiltrated the camps. They became part of the cat-and-mouse games of building teaching spaces only to see them torn down by soldiers. Many of the skills they picked up had little use as long as they were not allowed to sit exams or take up formal employment, but their English occasionally gave them a key to the world. Their language skills meant they could communicate with the occasional foreign diplomat or UN head who came to visit, relaying Rohingya demands and revealing their grievances, though they knew that came with risks. Those visits were often followed by a summoning to the offices of the camp authorities and a subsequent reprimand—at the least— even when those same authorities had encouraged the boys to speak as a way of parading the freedom Bangladesh had supposedly offered the refugees. Standing out, Zia realised, was a problem. If they were to stay, the Rohingya had to accept a life of restrictions and humiliation.

"We were not allowed to wear a nice t-shirt, nice shorts or nice pants", said Zia. "They can take us away or dishonour us in front of other people. 'You are a refugee, why are you wearing trousers?'

Their job is to control the Rohingya, their job is to destroy the Rohingya, their job is to force them to go back to Myanmar."

* * *

At first glance, from the outside, Kutupalong and Nayapara might not look so different to the Bangladeshi villages and small towns scattered around Cox's Bazar district. They sit just off Teknaf Road's market parades—filled with street hawkers, tea shops and chemists—little betraying what lies behind other than a proliferation of NGO logos. The entrances are discrete: brick roads that begin somewhere between the shops but then wind their way past NGO offices and checkpoints manned nonchalantly by local police; then on towards the main aid collection points; and, finally, the blocks of tin-roofed shelters.

Only rarely have I ever walked that road in Nayapara, almost identical to its counterpart in Kutupalong except that it lies flat rather than requiring a walk uphill. Almost always, we enter through the brick field to the south of the camp, where a red haze hangs in the air, resting on the shoulders of the dust-covered Rohingya and Bangladeshi labourers who form, bake, then shift, atop their heads, thousands of bricks per day. Its mosque is often empty outside of prayer times, providing a rare corner to talk without the attention of curious ears. There, I have often met Salim and Abdul Hakeem, young Nayapara teachers like Nobi, who fear always the attention of the intelligence services purely for educating other Rohingya. They take turns to talk while the other sits by the mosque window, watching for any unexpected arrivals and shooing away the children who, without anything else to do, always find themselves attracted to anything new. They share much with their cousins in Kutupalong: their families persisted through hardship and precarity in Bangladesh over what they felt was certain death in Myanmar; and both taught cohorts of refugees not even a generation

removed, instilling hope in them though they held little themselves. But Nayapara also has a noticeably more pronounced ten-
sion with the security apparatus and the local population. This is
perhaps because of all that is involved in living in Teknaf, it is a
place sparse in sustainable opportunity but abundant with criminal possibilities.

The Rohingya do not have passports or any other kind of
travel document; most do not have any type of identification; and
only a minority have UNHCR-registered refugee cards, which
hold little sway anyway. The Rohingya, for the most part, are
completely unable to cross borders unless they opt for routes
walked or sailed under the stewardship of a smuggler. A few
well-placed payments can land a refugee a Bangladeshi passport,
but the costs are beyond the means of most, so there is no question of the Rohingya being able to board a flight and seek asylum. Aside from returning to a country that, by this time, many
of them have never seen, there was only one orthodox route out
of Bangladesh—resettlement in a Western country. The places
where they were settled were often ones they had never heard
of—Bradford in the north of England, Carlow in rural Ireland,
parts of the United States with the bitterest of winters—away
from the global capitals where the more privileged diaspora of
Rohingya leaders in the 1980s had settled, but they offered a way
for the Rohingya to build new communities and delve into education and business.

Nobi was chosen for resettlement to the UK in 2010. His mind
came alive with the prospect of seeing a world beyond Nayapara,
of education pursued openly (rather than cloaked by a bedsheet)
and which he could put to practical use. Some of his friends had
already gone and they were thriving. Nobi prepared his family for
the exciting change, the first time hope had visited them in close
to two decades since they had left Myanmar. In his excitement, he
borrowed money from a Rohingya neighbour who had more than

most, fully expecting to repay the modest loan when he arrived in the UK, and set about buying what he thought the family needed—luggage and new clothes that did not have Nayapara's dust permanently embedded between the fibres. He dreamed of arriving in Bradford refreshed. A week before he was supposed to go, Bangladesh cancelled the resettlement process—including for everyone who had already been assigned. They claimed it would be a pull factor for more refugees.

"Opportunity found me, then kicked me at the last moment", Nobi said.

The blow knocked Nobi into a common Rohingya reality: debt. He thought he would quickly be able to pay off his creditor for the loan of $500, but was now not only jobless but also without any prospect of finding work. He became one of many. Debt is regularly accrued by families forking out to pay for dowries to marry their daughters off. Others borrow to bribe, through brokers, officials for documents like birth certificates or national identity cards that allow them to occasionally pose as people other than refugees. Larger amounts can build up for paying yet more brokers who help traffic people abroad, usually to Malaysia, Saudi Arabia or India. Sometimes they end up out of pocket simply because of extortion.

It was not that debt did not exist in Myanmar, but there they had ways to earn money. Before camp life largely flattened wealth, they could work for the well-off among them and many families at least had some land or livestock they could sell. In Bangladesh, they owned almost nothing, not even the soil their shelters sat upon. That made clearing their debts difficult—and potentially dangerous. Even those as well educated as Nobi, who can slip between several languages, could not formally work. Most would pass their ration card to the family they borrowed from and men could then provide simple supplies for the family, perhaps even chip slowly away at the debt by working as day labourers. Nobi turned to the River Naf and got a job on the

Bangladeshi boats that fished its waters. Instead of escaping to his dream of a more stable life, he ended up closer to Myanmar than he had ever been since leaving it as a child, while still knowing he could not really return. He was not just staring at its banks from the hills behind Nayapara any more, but floating on its waters and even, occasionally, forced to step on its soil. He had his reservations, but he had been married young and forced to learn that the responsibility of caring for his young wife meant taking the risk of venturing into a labour market that was hostile towards him. Permits from the Burmese military were required to fish the Naf's waters (it was not unusual for even Bangladeshi border guards to be shot at, accused of crossing the invisible boundary) and the Bangladeshis who employed Nobi often delegated the task to him. Though he did it many times, he was never able to feel comfortable walking into the office. To enter the office, he had to pass NaSaKa (security) soldiers lazing about intoxicated, pulling on cigarettes and leaning on their guns. He avoided locking eyes. It broke his heart. He was there on his own soil, in the country he had been born in, but was forced to identify as a Bangladeshi fisherman. It preyed on him through the working day, during the breaks when they waited for high tide to cast their nets, when his Bengali colleagues would sing fishermen's songs or laze about—but the pause in work let his mind wander towards questions about whether he could ever walk past those soldiers and be treated an equal in his homeland.

"It was heartbreaking", Nobi said. "This is my country, my motherland, where I was born and today I have to pretend I am a Bengali. Sometimes I sat for an hour asking myself: when will we be able to be citizens of our country?"

Fatima

While men can more readily offer their services as labourers in Bangladesh's fields or waters, Rohingya women have fewer options unless they enter domestic work in houses far beyond the camps. It is a dangerous option that could expose the women to abuse, or worse, from families they work for or the brokers who market their services. It is even more dangerous for the thousands of single mothers whose husbands were killed in Myanmar, smuggled to Malaysia or Saudi Arabia for work opportunities, or who simply abandoned their families for second wives—an unfortunately frequent occurrence.

Two of those things happened to Fatima,[1] who swings off her *niqab* as she walks into a friend's shelter—all the men are sent away. Our meeting has been organised by a mutual contact, Rafiq,[2] a Rohingya neighbour from the Kutupalong camp whom she has known since childhood. I have heard plenty about women in debt being forced to play roles in drug smuggling, but it was almost impossible to find someone willing to speak until Rafiq vouched for me. We sit down on the floor, under a red and yellow paisley-patterned sheet that adorns the ceiling to hide the tin roofing, a single lightbulb poking from between its folds— the almost universal single luxury a Rohingya refugee acquires over decades. The hosts point their small fan towards me in hospitality. Fatima has lived alone with her two children since her husband went to Malaysia in 2013, paying a *dalaal* (broker) $500 to facilitate the journey. It was supposed to be the family's route out of the camp's poverty of hope, but her husband turned it into something different. When he got to Malaysia, he abandoned Fatima. Within months he remarried and cut off all links, lumping her with the debt and a creditor he would never again have to face himself. To repay the loan, Fatima followed the usual path of passing on her ration card and then feeding her children by scraping together a small amount of money to buy rice from the local market in Kutupalong.

That was how Fatima ended up muling Yaba. The "madness pill", as it is known, is a mixture of methamphetamines and caffeine that pours out of Myanmar into Bangladesh and Thailand with an ease enjoyed by neither the Rohingya nor any of Myanmar's other marginalised frontier communities. For five years, Fatima lived with the debt. She did incentive work provided by NGOs specifically for women, soap-making or tailoring, that barely dented the sum but at least gave her a little to feed her three children. She bought her small rations at the teeming bazaar by the foot of Kutupalong, from a Bangladeshi shopkeeper. Rohingya were regular visitors to his shop, but rarely as customers. In need of some cash, they usually came to sell a portion of their aid supplies to him. So, when he saw that Fatima was regularly coming to buy, it occurred to him that she needed more money than she could get skimming a kilo of rice or lentils from the family's diet.

The shopkeeper was part of a chain that brought Yaba across the border into Bangladesh, then up to Cox's Bazar and on to Dhaka. There, it fed a rising addiction in the capital, especially in private universities where youth aspiring to break into the middle class took the pills in order to study for days without sleeping, or to the port city of Chittagong, where the brightly coloured, candy-like pills were mixed in with more legitimate cargo and shipped to distant destinations. It was not all that surprising given where they lived, at a gateway for the movement of goods across the border—both legal trade with Myanmar and the illicit movement of drugs and people. Bangladesh has long been aware of this trade. Dozens of checkpoints already lined the Teknaf Road, where buses and overloaded *tuk-tuks* would be stopped every few minutes and checked by soldiers or plainclothed officers. Every now and again, Bangladesh announced big busts, finding hauls of hundreds of thousands of pills packed in suitcases, or smaller amounts in school bags carried on the endless lines of buses constantly racing each other along Bangladesh's one-lane rural highways.

The shopkeeper asked Fatima to help him bypass these checkpoints. Other Rohingya women were known to be used as mules for more complicated tasks, such as carrying the drugs across the border on boats, but Fatima was being offered something more straightforward: to assume the shopkeeper's risk for around $20 per trip. Keep doing it, and she would soon be debt-free, he said. She accepted.

She dressed in black and pulled her *niqab* over her face for the short walk from the block of shelters for Kutupalong's registered refugees down to the main bazaar. The shopkeeper was waiting in an autorickshaw he had hired and took her up to the first checkpoint beyond Kutupalong where he handed Fatima a package for her to slip under the seat. She guessed she was carrying around 5,000 pills. She boarded a bus alone and prayed she was not suspected by any of the narcotics officers at the checkpoints on Teknaf Road, and then rode up to the main town in Ukhiya. Then she switched transport again and headed for Cox's Bazar, where she waited for the shopkeeper at the bus station, handed over the drugs and then made her way home.

"I was used as a labourer", said Fatima. "My duty was to take these pills from Kutupalong to Cox's Bazar. That's it."

On the third trip Fatima made under the shopkeeper's wing, still ignorant of his name, she arrived at the bus station in Cox's Bazar and looked around. Sat on the town's southern edge, it was chaotic: 100 buses crammed in on pavements and jostling to enter and exit and pass each other along a road that was supposed to accommodate all of this, and all traffic passing through Cox's Bazar, with one lane for each direction. Her ears drowned in the noise of teenage conductors banging the sides of bus exteriors entirely dimpled by dents, and of impatient passengers shouting in frustration. The passengers were local traders and students from villages shuttling along Teknaf Road, between colleges in town and their rural homes. Hidden among them may have been some Rohingya, also returning from studies or even work in Chittagong, far enough from Cox's Bazar for the unscrupulous foremen of construction sites or the city's notorious shipbreaking yards to not care about reporting a refugee to the police. Some may have been even doing the exact same job as Fatima, muling narcotics for the people who wanted its profits without its risks. She scanned through this image of chaos, but could not see the shopkeeper anywhere. From the pocket of her black cloak, she withdrew a simple mobile phone and dialled the number he had given her for this trip, the latest in a string of numbers he had burned through in the few weeks she had known him.

Their exchanges had been few and brief and so when the phone connected to a man who was not her shopkeeper, Fatima did not notice enough difference in his voice to warrant concern or to conceal the purpose of the call. She told him she had arrived with the package. The voice on the other end told her to wait where she was. After half an hour, a car halted abruptly in front of her and out jumped four men she did not know. They bundled her into the car and drove straight off. They took her to a house somewhere in the city and chucked her into a darkened room, then confiscated the package and locked the door. They bound her hands with rope and beat her with a bamboo stick. For a day she was kept in the darkness, scared she would die at the hands of these men who kept threatening her unless she told them who had given her the drugs. She had no answer for them. But they relented. The next day, suddenly, they told her she was free to leave and she phoned a relative who worked as a rickshaw rider in Cox's Bazar.

The anonymous shopkeeper, who had not been there to help her, wasted no time in finding Fatima's shelter once she returned. He wanted to know where his pills were and when she told him the story, he demanded Fatima swear by Allah and the Qur'an that she had not stolen the drugs herself. She never saw him again, not even in the market.

"It was just a business to him", said Fatima. "I didn't matter."

* * *

The Bangladeshi press, especially in the Cox's Bazar area, have long accused the Rohingya of criminality. They amplify the myths of the Rohingya as responsible for spreading HIV within Bangladesh, or of the camps as hotbeds of terrorist recruitment. Many around the country have come to believe the Yaba trade does not just feed off the Rohingya camps but exists because of them, an impression passed on to the nation by a local media easily manipulated by the powerful locals who actually have stakes in these trades. When the Rohingya fled again for Bangladesh in 2017, the idea that many of them were carrying Yaba with them became a national obsession. A commander of the Rapid Action Battalion for Cox's Bazar at the time told me Yaba was a Rohingya "personal possession", a sort of currency they hoped to trade. In his mind, the people who said they left their homes and every-thing in them to burn, who had stumbled through swampy fields on the border carrying on their backs little more than their elderly, those people had prioritised finding their bag of drugs over everything else. The reality of the Rohingya role has often been more similar to Fatima's: as smaller, disposable cogs within a system that connected the far more powerful on either side of the border. Even those who transported the drugs across the bor-der were no more than go-betweens, assuming the risk at a bor-der rather than a checkpoint.

The drugs are made in remote corners of Myanmar (places even its watchful military cannot maintain complete control over) and then carried down from the Myanmar highlands by ethnic Rakhine, who enjoy more freedom to move than the Rohingya but are similarly starved for opportunity. A Rohingya boy jailed by Bangladesh for carrying Yaba explained how busi-nessmen then take the drugs off the Rakhine transporters and look for impoverished young Rohingya, offering them far more than they could earn as labourers in several months, to carry the drugs into Bangladesh. Tasked with carrying up to 4,000 pills each, the boys originally carried them in bags or by hand. As Bangladeshi police became more vigilant, they turned to swallowing plastic bags filled with their valuable contraband. They would go to the border and take boats or sneak through foliage before heading to cities like Chittagong or handing the pills on to men like the Bangladeshi shopkeeper who handled Fatima and probably countless other Rohingya who had been born refugees in Bangladesh.

Bakthiar Ahmed was one such person. He was also a shopkeeper in Kutupalong bazar and a council member for the immediate locality, but his real power was in his land. His plots off Teknaf Road, just south of the bazar, were not themselves very valuable, but since the 1990s they had become the overflow site for Kutupalong, hosting the uncounted refugees who were invisible to the state. If the situation in the main camp was bad, with a whole "lost generation" deprived of work or education, then it was even worse in the makeshift camps ruled over by Bakthiar. Though the government turned back as many boats as it could, the camps had grown through a constant trickle and then sudden bursts triggered when parts of Rakhine would come under attack. Yet it refused to acknowledge the camp population and banned the aid agencies who supported the refugees. The population became known as the "hunger refugees". For Bakthiar, this was the ideal recruiting ground for the young men, and sometimes women, he needed to probably mule Yaba.

He lived by the roadside—the camp arcing around his spacious home, eating into the forest behind it. Set against the dense forest, the camp was a jarring image of dusty hills carrying an incomprehensible number of bamboo and tarpaulin homes. By 2017, this image would be cloned across a much larger space, when suddenly it was the sight of greenery that would be rarer. When I first visited Kutupalong in 2015, to meet the families of the sons of this forsaken settlement who had disappeared in their thousands, it was with Bakthiar that I had to sit for a lunch of buffalo curry and seek permission. He was known as Member Sahab—the type of deferential title used for the local politician of every little hamlet in the country—and bragged about how he helped the Rohingya by letting them stay on his land. Long-bearded and dressed like a religious man, he also boasted of his great relationship with some of the religiously affiliated Turkish aid groups, who he said wanted to take him to Turkey to fulfil his dream of meeting then-Prime Minister Recep Tayyip Erdoğan. He presented his son, apparently an aspiring journalist, and asked whether I could find him a job. After holding court, when I set off around the camps, a Rohingya employee accompanied me. The son shadowed, though not with the intention of learning how to interview.

The houses were packed tighter than even those that would come with the arrivals of 2017. The homes, only a few feet wide, almost sat upon one another and extended families were crammed into them. Without any meaningful aid presence, the infrastructure was completely neglected. Sewage systems were absent and so human waste trickled between tents, mixing with the slush the earth they lived on became when it rained. Water pumps and toilets existed wherever someone had put them, perhaps by a charity working without permission and certainly without planning.

Bakthiar was not just a landowner or a politician: he was gatekeeper to the camp, though he preferred to think of himself as a protector. The reality was that he controlled the lives of its inhabitants and any access to them. Few talk freely about him in Kutupalong, but Rohingya who live abroad, away from his informants, are not short of words to describe him. One Rohingya now living in Malaysia said he had seen the politician allow charities to disperse cash bursaries outside his home, only to confiscate some of the money from the refugees when the charity workers had left. They also claimed that when couples visited him in his shop in Kutupalong market to lodge complaints or seek his help, Bakthiar would regularly take the woman away to a room above his shop, leaving her husband waiting. Suspicions about this politician and of others, more high-ranking than him, in illicit trades involving the Rohingya, have never gone away. While he controlled access to the informal camps for visitors, traffickers involved in everything from drugs to brokering trips to Malaysia, Saudi Arabia or India and the outright snatching of children and women for domestic work or as sex workers—in Cox's Bazar or as far as India—seemed to operate freely.

The supply of young Rohingya who could be convinced or exploited by the brokers never stopped. The Rohingya who had returned to Myanmar found that the safety promised by Bangladesh and UNHCR did not exist and that the military occupation they had fled in 1991 was not isolated. It was the beginning of a new normal. Forced labour continued and a new security force, the NaSaKa, was set up in 1992. The name of this purported border force, focused entirely on northern Rakhine, invariably fell out of the mouths of newcomers to Bangladesh describing the fresh violence they were fleeing. Though still relatively small, the force was frequently described as drunken and brutal. Human Rights Watch documented a case of inebriated NaSaKa soldiers taking a young Rohingya woman from her home and raping her through the night, repeatedly for five nights, until she fled to Bangladesh with her family.[3] Others arrived with stories of children going missing with frightening regularity, never to be seen again unless as bodies discarded in the bushes.

Throughout the 2000s, the Rohingya became a more permanent object of the military government's fury, which also increasingly seeped into the wider population's sentiment against the Muslim minority. Intercommunal clashes became common, sending small waves into Bangladesh, which would try to repel them despite a metronomic rhythm of localised attacks by the military or Rakhine neighbours on individual villages, ensuring there was an almost constant flow of refugees who ended up in the makeshift camps.

The worst of these clashes came in 2012. A Rakhine woman was murdered and the facts were quickly repackaged as a rumour that spread through the state of her being robbed and raped by a group of Rohingya, though both the rape and identity of the suspects was later questioned by an investigation. In retaliation, a group of Muslim missionaries from Yangon was burned to death in their bus. For months, Rakhine was set ablaze and Sittwe, specifically, torn apart by violence that displaced the city's entire Rohingya population. Villages in the surrounding areas feared what was coming and began to leave. Some went to Bangladesh, others to Malaysia.

The UN estimated that around 200,000 Rohingya were living in Bangladesh between the repatriation of the 1990s and October 2016, though the exact number is hard to judge. Hiding in the unregistered camp or among local populations, or even in the forest, was the safest thing to do when Bangladesh's policy was to push back Rohingya who arrived on its borders and to repatriate anyone already there. Some stayed only temporarily, long enough to connect with brokers who could transport them elsewhere, to places they heard there was work and freedom to move, while those same journeys encouraged those already in the camps to disappear without leaving a mark on the records.

PART 2

6

THE BAY OF BENGAL

Suliman (May 2015)

Nestled between the fingers of each man crouching under the low ceiling of a tearoom in Bakthiar's domain is a scrap borrowed from the corner of a newspaper. Each slip is marked with phone numbers beginning in +66 or +60—the country codes for calling Thailand and Malaysia. They are not treasured but always guarded. If they could, every man in this room—and the women elsewhere whose fingers grip similar scrawls—would burn them. It would mean freedom from their anguish and uncertainty. As it is, they phone the numbers often, expecting no voice on the other end.

Making that apparently futile call is their only way of contacting the traffickers holding their children and husbands deep in the jungle along the treacherous Thai-Malaysian border. Most of them are there having tried to get from Myanmar or Bangladesh to Malaysia, where they have heard of a country that promises escape from the open-air prisons of besieged villages and refugee camps. Others have been given no say in the matter. But their situation has been complicated. In the days before I visit these men, the first time I arrive in Kutupalong, these trafficking rings have suddenly been forced under an intense media and political spotlight that has startled the traffickers into deserting their boats at sea and abandoning their human cargo. According to the UN, at least 4,000 people are adrift somewhere between the Bay of Bengal and the Andaman Sea. Many of their families have not heard from their children for months, since they slipped away from their homes, and now fear they may never talk again. Any contact comes in snatches between lashings delivered live over the phone, so that all they can hear is the victims begging their families to scratch together inordinate ransoms demanded by the traffickers. Others are sent pictures and videos of the torture. The families beg for mercy but are met with silence. The traffickers only resume contact when they feel that silence has bred enough anxiety for their demands to be met.

The thin-framed, bony-faced Suliman is the only man in that tearoom who has not had any contact with the traffickers at all. He has tried but found no way through. His son Mohammed Rafique has been gone a month, not long since he turned 18. For weeks, his proposed departure had fuelled family debates, arguments held within the confines of their shelter, so close to each other they felt the force of breath exhaled by raised voices. It spans only 2m^2, an entire wall taken up by the stacks of firewood Suliman has collected, built on Bakthiar's land not long after the 2012 riots, when they finally felt a lifetime of Myanmar's injustices had become unbearable. Though his eldest son had already been in Malaysia for several years, his journey paid for by the father of the Bangladeshi woman he married soon after leaving Myanmar, Suliman was hesitant for another of his sons to go. The journey had become more dangerous, lined with more stops and involving more brokers and traffickers intent on leeching money. But the family had nothing. His children could not study and he found only sporadic work that paid at most 50 taka

($0.60) a day. As unregistered refugees, they were given no aid. Mohammed Rafique's mother had been looking for a bride for the boy, who was well within the age bracket in which many young Rohingya get married, but could find no one. Age was making the manual tasks of the house difficult for her and it was typical for a daughter-in-law to help. Their son thought money earned abroad might make marriage more likely. The argument eventually swayed Suliman and, when he yielded, it took little time to put the journey together. Boats were departing almost daily and he could leave as soon as the broker was paid a deposit.

Mohammed Rafique had been preceded by neighbours. He still went despite many of them having gone missing. Suliman's friend Syed Alam's son had gone eight months earlier, and though he had paid a ransom he had received no confirmation of his son's arrival. Though notoriously dangerous, these boat journeys had remarkably little stigma surrounding them. Many young Rohingya slipped away from their homes without telling their parents, fearing they might object, but it was also not unusual for families to pay for their sons to go to Malaysia in the hope that there they would be able to work and send money home. The boats had been going since the 1990s, but over time the system had become more complicated as it grew and morphed into an organism accommodating ever-increasing numbers of people trying to draw profit from it.

The fuel for this machine were Rohingya youth, mostly male, who had tired of the conditions they lived in. The 2012 riots in Sittwe had left the city's Rohingya caged in displacement camps they could not escape, while in the countryside they were paralysed both by fear and the very real tightening of the military's grip. Students at Sittwe's university found those facilities cut off because being caught anywhere in the city beyond the camps was enough for them to be arrested. Education was not just a path towards a career or socio-economic progression; it was resistance, a way to ensure the Rohingya continued their existence and could fight for themselves. If they were not allowed to pursue the careers their qualifications merited, then at least they could teach the next generation. The new reality was suffocating. Some of them took the usual escape route—to Bangladesh—but they found the only places open to them were the crowded shanty towns in the forests around Kutupalong and Nayapara, where they would have to hustle for every meal, unrecognised as refugees and beyond the reach of humanitarian organisations. Since 2010, Sheikh Hasina's government had banned even the trickles of irregular aid, describing it as a pull factor for more refugees. But the camps were still swelling beyond capacity because it was not aid but safety that pulled them into Bangladesh, even though the new arrivals saw people like Suliman living in destitution, stripped of the traditional means of living from the land and water. A few could settle into a fisherman's life among Bangladeshis, but this depended on the acceptance of local communities.

Those new arrivals found the reality of Bangladeshi daily life hardly better than what they had left—a place where family and social pressures all heaved on top of each other. The disturbed and frustrating lives of young Rohingya who could not even remember Myanmar were testimony to this. Meanwhile, friends who had gone abroad relayed the good parts about jobs and freedom to roam, and the brokers found it useful to repeat that message. The same story was sold on both sides of the river. Every camp or village had its own localised *dalaal*, the word given to the men who brokered the legal and the illegal and who were often full-blown traffickers. The workers at the base of this elaborate structure—tasked with making the first connection, selling the dream—operated freely throughout Bangladesh, and though some were traffickers involved in the dirtiest sides of this informal industry others were simply present as an ordinary, even crucial, element of the social fabric. Their first contacts were often with cousins, nephews and in-laws as a plug into a system that made things move. For villagers unaccustomed to government machinery, the *dalaal* opened doors already ajar, took fees to push past official corruption or to obscure bureaucracy, securing something as simple as an ID card or passport that should need no intermediary. They recruited people to promises of prosperity even when legal routes were available, either charging them when there should be no fee or inventing quicker but irregular routes to work in places like Saudi Arabia. So, when Sittwe exploded in 2012, they prospered.

For many, the Bangladesh option simply did not appeal and their resolve to move on was exploited by traffickers who turned the region into a hub, exporting not only its own tired refugees but also some who hoped Bangladesh would be only a transit. Those privy to the dangers of the sea journey and realities of life in Malaysia were offered passage to India, which was close and offered a humble but stable existence, or Saudi Arabia. Successful Rohingya from past migrations had established themselves in the Gulf kingdom, where a sympathetic King Abdullah had offered residencies to Rohingya who found ways to the kingdom. The *dalaals* helped by fixing passports and *Umrah* pilgrimage visas that could be discarded on arrival. Residency permits were provided, as promised, and they were given the security to work freely and in stable employment so they could send money home.

The rest were convinced that the risks of Malaysia were worth it and that it was an opportunity that could be secured for only a small fee, or even for free, on condition that the debt was repaid once they arrived in Malaysia and found a job. The brokers insisted that finding a job and comfort were inevitable. Once the agreement was made, these brokers plugged the aspirant traveller into the vast transnational network that had grown fat feeding off the Rohingya.

But not all chose to go. As the machine grew, so did the greed. In a corner of Bangladesh, where opportunities were scarce and proximity to Myanmar made the smuggling of Yaba pills and other contraband a lucrative business, there was also an appetite for trading in people. On Shah Porir Dwip, the silty southernmost tip of Bangladesh that reaches out into the Bay of Bengal, large villas at odds with their isolated environment sprouted among forestry. These were not the homes of fishermen any longer. As a gateway to the sea, and close enough to Myanmar that it could be transformed into an assembly point for the traffickers and their victims, Shah Porir Dwip's once impoverished villagers had found riches. But feeding this appetite required the business to keep running and, as more sought ways in, for it to grow. That meant boats needed to be moving all the time. Already operating in the shadows of the law, Teknaf became a more dangerous place, somewhere you could disappear and be shipped off before anyone noticed. Being on the roads after dark was a risk. The traffickers needed to fill the boats, to ensure the big fees taken from ransoms were made, so they took who they could and it did not matter whether they paid anything up front. The Rohingya were the perfect target; already scared of reporting crimes to the police, they certainly would not dare accuse the local communities of kidnapping their children.

Zia

Though he felt his face finally freed from the blindfold digging into his skin, Zia still saw darkness. He was not gagged, but remained silent. He had not spoken since the men who grabbed him on the outskirts of Kutupalong silenced his struggles with their fists and the threat of their guns. Now he was being held in the dark, somewhere he did not recognise, by men he did not know. He had already been on edge, concerned about repercussions for his advocacy. Only a week earlier he had been stopped by police when travelling between Nayapara and Kutupalong, so he wondered whether this was another attempt to intimidate him. They kept Zia waiting in the darkness for three hours and then hauled him to his feet, prodding him along for a 30-minute walk down to the river, where a small boat waited. Already on the boat were fifteen men, mostly Rohingya and some Bangladeshis, as well as three traffickers. Zia was told to board. The boat sat on the water for two days, its captive passengers given no indication of what their immediate future would be. They were given no food or water. On the second night, under the cover of more darkness, the boat began to meander down the Naf towards the Bay of Bengal.

Sitting offshore, fishing trawlers waited for the cargo shuttled to them by boats like the one Zia was sitting on. They sat out of sight of the Bangladeshi coastguard (or where those eyes chose not to see), waiting for days, even weeks, as their passengers were discreetly brought aboard in small batches. The boat Zia was loaded onto held 310 people. Others held as many as 600 on trawlers designed for only a crew of fishermen and their haul. They had been brought on much smaller fishing boats from Rohingya villages or at various inconspicuous points along the Bangladeshi coast. Most were Rohingya, but many were impoverished Bengali villagers who had come from opposite ends of the country, sometimes in full knowledge of where they were going and at other times expecting to be set up with a job in a Cox's Bazar resort.

They were packed in so tightly that all had to sit and sleep upright, shoulders rubbing against each other. The composition of the trafficking crews varied. Sometimes Rohingya or Bengalis were among them, often used as translators or enforcers for the captains, but the rest were often unknown to the travellers, who guessed at Burmese or Thai. Sometimes they described them as "magh", an old term still used by the Rohingya for ethnic Rakhine. The food the crew provided was scant and basic, often little more than steamed rice given once a day. Some of the passengers supplemented it with puffed rice they had brought themselves—if the crews had allowed them to take anything aboard. The women were kept on a separate deck, near the captain's room, into which the youngest of the women occasionally disappeared.

Most of the passengers had only a basic education, if any, but even Zia knew little of the geography they were passing through. The journey was a long haul of seas he could not identify and days and weeks that merged into one another. Sometimes the boat suddenly stopped, when the engine switched off after the crew received news of coastguard teams on alert. These were teams that had either not been bribed or had been sent to make a show of their work because of media scrutiny following, perhaps, the previous capsizing of a boat somewhere along the route. The boat's load intermittently lightened when a passenger succumbed to sickness and was thrown into the sea. Zia felt himself getting weaker, his muscles wasting away. He avoided speaking up after he watched the traffickers lash at other passengers with bamboo canes. There were only eight traffickers and, even with their weapons, all the passengers should have been able to overpower them, but the food they had been given was sufficient only for bare survival.

The same route had been taken by so many others before, those who had chosen to and those who had not. Zia's childhood friend Abdul Goni also unwittingly ended up adrift on the sea, forced onto a boat by criminals who tricked him by offering him labour work on a paddy field but instead locked him and a dozen others in an abandoned house. Barely a word was said to the men, who feared local Bangladeshis anyway and knew any kind of fight would probably end badly for them. The police would hardly take their side when they were so far from the camp, engaged in the illegal act of seeking a living. The men instead phoned Abdul Goni's wife, who could not meet their demands. So Abdul Goni, like Zia, was sold to the traffickers.

Asmida

Asmida Begum also did not know where she was going. She spent her weeks on the upper deck reserved for women, slouched under the unnerving gaze of the captain and his team. She had ended up on the boat without ever making a decision. All she had done was run. At the time, she didn't know where, or from what, she was running—just that generations of Rohingya before her had taught her that the raucous arrival of Burmese soldiers meant she had to put distance between herself and her village. Hers was the panicked escape of a child who had heard the darkest stories of what Burmese soldiers do to young girls, and feared becoming their next victim as their trucks screeched to a halt outside her village and bullets rattled the air. She was 15 and with a group of girls her age who were also swept up in that terror-stricken stampede that separated Asmida from her entire family. The girls followed the crowd to the river nearby and automatically joined others bundling onto a waiting boat. But instead of finding safety, each stroke of the boatman's oar signed an implicit contract with the passengers. Their reprieve would only deliver them to more exploitation. Like the boat that Zia had been forced to board on the River Naf, this flimsy vessel carried the villagers far beyond their homes, downstream towards the sea, towards the floating fleet in the Bay of Bengal. Only when Asmida was transferred onto the packed trawler was she informed of her destination.

"We didn't speak much but we did occasionally, in very low voices", she said. "I saw some of my villagers here and saw that the men did not get enough food. So I tried to keep something aside for the others." Besides, she struggled to keep down whatever she did eat because of the boat's constant rocking. "No one was allowed to move anywhere. I was given one place to sit in and I had to stay there, just sitting. There was not even space to lie down and sleep. Four of us would sit and another four of us would try to sleep, lying on top of each other."

After two months of a journey that halted almost every time they got going, the trawler approached Thailand. At night, once again, they were loaded onto rubber dinghies and rowed towards the Thai coastal area of Ranong, navigating the mangrove roots that jutted upwards out of the water until their boats nestled on a beach. They were guided immediately into the jungle and told to ascend a hill. There, they found the first holding camp. In some places there were just open spaces, or a little tarpaulined covering. The arrivals were sorted into various groups, given wristbands that identified the next trafficker they were going to be sold on to. Asmida posed a problem. She had no way of contacting her family. She did not even know yet that her father had drowned as he ran from the raiding soldiers. There was no ransom to be wrung from her.

Over the next seven days the traffickers moved the arrivals between the various camps they had established on mountaintops, sitting when calm and initiating new treks when informers updated them on the army's movements. They had been activating contacts built during their many years of selling Rohingya to find someone that might know Asmida, who might be willing to pay for her. They eventually came across a young man from her village.

"We spoke", said Asmida. "He said he'd save me by giving the money to the traffickers. So I agreed to get married. Those like me who had no contacts, no relatives, there was not much to pay. My husband paid only 30,000 baht because I didn't have any relatives. I didn't have anything. The brokers just wanted to arrange to sell me to someone. The broker came and said if you choose to do this it's easier, I'll make my money."

Money was what Ranong's camps existed for. If Teknaf had developed an economy based on Rohingya flesh, then Ranong was little different. A town on the other side of the border from Myanmar, similarly separated by a river that juts in from the sea, its mangrove forests were a safe haven for the traffickers. They used it as a hub for contacting buyers, informing them that their "black chicken" had arrived, as they referred to the Rohingya and Bangladeshis. Girls like Asmida were sold on as quickly as possible. Men were sold on to other traffickers or into labour, sometimes sent back onto trawlers as slaves helping pull shrimp from the sea. The rest would be shunted between one camp and another for days, even weeks, before they were eventually moved away from Ranong, loaded onto trucks heading for Songkhla near Malaysia. There they were held until their families paid ransoms that could easily reach $3,000. Where Teknaf was a wild, lawless scramble that sustained the business—a place to simply ensure enough people were being heaved onto the boats—Thailand was the network's pivot, where the money was secured.

After two weeks in Ranong, Zia was still being bounced between camps, "kept like a fish". He had been able neither to bathe nor to change clothes during the month spent at sea, and in Ranong he still sat in those same clothes he had been snatched in, his thin white shirt now tattered and putrid. His purposely groomed hair had grown into a wavy mass, weighed down by sweat, and a slight beard now framed his face. His body had wasted away and his eyes were now constantly red. When he was fed, the rice had a strange smell as if something had been mixed into it to dull their senses. He saw thousands of Rohingya hidden among the trees, penned in under the forest canopy with little more space than they had been afforded on the boats.

By 5 October 2014, he was being moved again. It was 4 am and more than 100 in the group were being shepherded by two traffickers, one leading the way and the other at the rear ensuring no one slipped away. After half an hour of this, their tired bodies forced to wade through waters at various points, the traffickers stopped them in an open space. But the moment of respite was brief. Suddenly there was the sound of gunfire. A team of armed police swooped in, grabbed the traffickers and arrested all present.

* * *

Through all these years of trafficking, during its unbridled growth, there had scarcely been any attempt to look into this industrial-scale movement of people by any of the countries it touched—not by Thailand or Malaysia, nor Bangladesh, and certainly not Myanmar. They could hardly plead ignorance; the signs were there. The Thai navy would occasionally tow a ship back out to sea, provide the refugees with a few rations and leave them, which would get a little attention on outlets like Al Jazeera. Every few months, Bangladeshi media would report on a heavily loaded boat capsizing in the Bay of Bengal. The passengers recovered by the country's coastguard were always a mixture of Bangladeshis and Rohingya. In Malaysia, local journalist S. Arulldas began a lonely, frightening search for the camps when he noticed a string of cases involving the brutal deaths of people no one could identify, their bodies found dumped in plantations and rivers. In the media, they became known as boat people, as if these journeys of a few weeks defined their humanity. For these boat people, apparently, it was natural to be on the sea, untethered to any nation. None of this ever drew more than a collectively raised eyebrow. There was no discussion about who moved these people or why so many had boarded boats, no thought given to how systematic it was. No one wanted to look too closely at the roles of military men and local politicians who had more wealth than they should have. The network revealed itself by accident, because the traffickers went too far. Their impunity had fed greed, and had encouraged a carelessness and complacency that meant they pushed the limits of their exploitation, using violence casually to extort money from families who had already paid, or whose children had already died, and to settle scores with each other.

For years, Hajj Ismail had been asked to confront this brutality, forced to reconcile its existence with his own powerlessness to stop it. He had lived in Bangkok for more than twenty years, having been made a political exile for his small role in Myanmar's 8888 movement/uprising. He knew many of the major players in Thailand, including some of the Rohingya involved in the trade of their own people. That was why families came to him and his organisation, the Rohingya Peace Network in Thailand, to negotiate on their behalf whenever an impasse had been reached with the traffickers. The last time he had taken on this task, the traffickers had been holding two young Rohingya boys, and although the ransom had been paid they were refusing to release them unless more money was given. But the mediation had not worked. The family could not afford to pay any more, so the traffickers had killed the boys. Enraged, the family persuaded Hajj Ismail that more needed to be done. He had previously spoken to the media about the conditions in these camps, but now he took them evidence: pictures and videos that the traffickers sent to families to extort money from them. The media buzz helped propel more action from the Thai authorities. Though there had been occasional raids like the one Zia had been caught in, months—sometimes a year—could pass between them, even though on one occasion security forces had found 2,000 Rohingya in a single raid. Then, on 30 April 2015, the Thai authorities announced they had found thirty bodies in a mass grave near the border.

Suddenly, the thin veil the traffickers had hidden behind was stripped away and the Thai authorities launched a full-blown operation. Less than a month later, Malaysia announced it had also found mass graves, in Wang Kelian, on its side of the same mountain where Thailand had found bodies. In reality, Malaysia had known about the camp since January 2015. Dozens of these camps existed on either side of this porous border, often demarcated by little more than barbed wire among the forestry. The traffickers had worked with such impunity that they had not thought much about covering their tracks, essentially operating in the open with the support of their environment. In the unruly Thai south, which had seen decades of civil war, locals were key to the business. These were areas where people, forgotten by the state, made money moving items desired and required over boundaries, whether legal or not. For a long time that had shifted whole tankers of petrol, which was much cheaper in Malaysia across the border. Trading humans was easier. Even locals not directly involved operated as sharp-eyed lookouts, informing the traffickers whenever a stranger had been spotted in their usually undisturbed enclave. It helped, as well, that they were able to pay off the people who were meant to be responsible for stopping the trafficking, including Manas Kongpaen, a lieutenant general in the Thai navy. Kongpaen's official role in the navy was to ensure he protected the "boat people" who arrived on Thailand's shores, a protection occasionally expressed by pulling them back out to sea so that Thailand could make clear its desire that neither Rohingya nor anyone else would be encouraged to turn up on its coast. But his riches were made by ignoring these orders. Instead of intercepting these arrivals, he facilitated the movement of the traffickers who paid him to ensure they were not disturbed when transporting their victims on the road from Ranong down to Songkhla. He fell into the business after he was posted to Ranong in 2010 and met a businessman who used the seafood trade as a cover for trafficking. Others had similar utility to the traffickers: the mayor of a region near the border and Pajjuban Angchotephan, a wealthy businessman known as the "godfather of Koh Lipe", a Thai island close to Malaysia where the refugees occasionally arrived.

As monstrous as this machine was, these well-placed contacts who had bought into it ensured it operated smoothly and beyond borders. Everyone involved was happy and, beyond them, no one else seemed concerned enough to pry too much. When a camp was occasionally stumbled across and closed down by the security forces before 2015, the captives would, mysteriously, end up back with the traffickers. The system, however, began to eat itself through the same greed it had grown on. No one did anything without profit and though their margins had grown rapidly, so had the numbers eager to take their slice. So, they became more brutal, killing captives they could not extract more from and killing each other in petty feuds. Until 2015, they had got away with it, but their brutality was ultimately what turned attention to them and when it came time to testify, they would talk as if they had done nothing wrong.

These discoveries and the steps the Southeast Asian countries suddenly took threw the trafficking network into disarray. Everywhere from the Bay of Bengal to the Malacca Strait, boats sat unguided. The traffickers were used to stopping only for the monsoon seasons that made the waters unnavigable but they initially tried to sit out this premature storm as well, hoping they would be able to resume their activities once the attention died down. Others abandoned their ships and their captives, sometimes even destroying the engines as a final cruelty. Floating on the sea these boats terrified the navies of Thailand, Malaysia and Indonesia, who all towed the boats back to sea whenever they approached. One boat was turned away by both Indonesia and Malaysia, its passengers condemned to death by governments who seemed content with a new mass grave aboard a trawler in the sea, as long as it was not within their forests. Each navy that towed them out provided rations that were quickly used up, so the stranded passengers drank salt water that failed to quench their thirst and only made them sicker. Stuck in international waters, the rate of deaths quickened and the passengers feared not a single one of them would survive. The strongest swimmers took turns wading out into the sea, creating a search radius around the boat as they looked for someone to rescue them. They went as far as they could and returned before they tired, repeating the task despite their lack of energy until one of them was found by an Indonesian fisherman from Aceh, on the north-west coast of Sumatra. Guided back to the boat, the fisherman was shocked by the sight. He picked up the radio Acehnese fish-ermen used to warn each other of dangers on the seas and soon had summoned a small flotilla of colleagues who towed the boat back to Indonesia, defying their government.

Zia

Loaded onto the lorry alongside the rest of the captives, Zia faced yet another journey he had not anticipated. He was beyond the control of the trafficking network that had first seized him in Bangladesh, transferred him to boats and then brought him into these Thai borderlands, but he had no reason to trust the police. He and the others sat silently as the vehicles rattled down to a detention centre, where they were ordered to sit on the floor—as rescued trafficking victims always were, whether in Bangladesh, Malaysia or Thailand—and separated into groups of Rohingya and Bangladeshis. The officers asked whether anyone spoke English, and Zia volunteered. His skills were invaluable to them. There were dozens of people to interview, all with stories of varying horror from the moment they had boarded the boats to landing in the Thai jungles. He heard stories like his and stories that were worse, translating them for investigators who found themselves with a trove of rapidly piling evidence against the traffickers and leads that suggested there was more to investigate. They decided to return to where they had seized Zia, to verify the stories they had been told, and took him to guide them through the sites he had stayed, to explain how these rudimentary encampments functioned in a smuggling scheme that was clearly more sophisticated than it appeared.

Helping the police and courts to expose part of the trafficking network, which ultimately helped towards the discovery of the mass graves, worked in Zia's favour. The Thai government officially recognised him as a victim of trafficking and he was registered by UNHCR. He was assigned to a shelter, where he was told there was a chance he might finally be resettled and escape the hopelessness he had known his whole life. But the shelter was in Songkhla, the remote area near the Thai border where he would have ended up anyway if the traffickers had not been caught while moving him between camps. None of the officers he had helped were nearby, nor were the Thai anti-trafficking activists he had got to know. His only connection to the outside world was through a single landline that he could not really use without the shelter's management monitoring him. It did not take long for him to feel unsafe. There were a few Burmese in the shelter whom he did not trust, especially as he still feared retribution from the human traffickers he had helped investigate. He also quickly noticed that Rohingya kept disappearing from the camp. One of the officers had used his position at the shelter to feed Rohingya back to the traffickers and insisted he could help Zia by giving him the number of a man who would take him to Malaysia and organise work and accommodation without paying a single penny. Only two weeks after he arrived, he saw the officer beating another of the Rohingya who had refused his offer, berating him for refusing to go to Malaysia. The boy's dreams of resettlement were not going to happen, the man shouted, nor was there any chance of him going back to Myanmar or Bangladesh. He would be stuck unless he took the trafficker's offer.

The exchange shook Zia, who had been given repeated promises from UNHCR officials about resettlement without any timetable towards making it happen. Without a phone, he had no way to complain about what was going on at the shelter and was worried about becoming the officer's next victim. Zia decided, with another Rohingya boy, that once midnight fell they would chance an escape. In the dark, they rushed into the trees and for three hours followed a road through the jungle, walking under the cover of the bush beside it, until they heard the call to prayer at a local mosque. Tired and hungry, they sought respite in that mosque, where the congregation took pity on them. While a worshipper scuttled off to find some food, they rested in the corner. They would have happily stayed there because it was the first generosity they had experienced in months. But the locals warned the boys not to linger too long. The eyes and ears of the traffickers were aware of everything. A local let Zia phone his uncle, who told him to get to another, larger mosque near the border.

One of the pitying worshippers at the first mosque offered Zia and his friend a short ride before releasing them back into the jungle to embark on the long trek towards Malaysia. Again, they stayed off the road to avoid eyes they could not trust, until eventually they reached the place where Zia was supposed to meet his uncle. It was much busier than expected. There were Muslims from all over Asia, apparently participating in some sort of conference, which allowed Zia and his friend to blend in and take advantage of the food on offer. They stayed a couple of days, but as the crowds thinned a Pakistani man took a special interest in

Zia. He was not a visitor to the border areas and, like the shelter supervisor, clearly had a stake in the trafficking game. He offered to help Zia get into Malaysia, but when the boys refused the man disappeared. A few hours later, police were at the mosque. The boys jumped from the window and tried to return to the darkened forests where they had spent so much of their time since stepping off the boats in Ranong. They ran but could not outrun the officers, who caught them and hauled them away. They were not taken to the police station.

Instead, they were driven towards the border until they arrived at a group of huts and crude structures. It was another trafficking camp, run by the Pakistani man who had seen in Zia an opportunity he was not willing to miss. The man thrust a phone into Zia's hands and demanded he ring his mother. He did as he was told but his mother, as desperate as she was to ensure Zia's safety, had nothing to give. After three hours, they had already tired of having Zia around and decided their best way to make a profit from him was by getting him into Malaysia and selling him on to another set of traffickers. Two Thai men turned up and Zia and the other Rohingya boy were forced to jump on the back of their motorbikes, which took them to the border. They were told to climb through a hole into the next human trafficking camp. It was another house filled with more miserable detainees. Outside it rained; inside the mosquitos attacked their flesh. Zia asked to use a phone—he wanted to contact someone in the UN or one of the journalists he'd known in Thailand—but the traffickers refused unless he was willing to call Bangladesh again. Defeated, he slumped back down and waited, as he was now used to, for the fate that would be decided by the men who believed they owned him. For six hours they waited until two more police officers told the boys to get inside a car. After eight hours the car stopped and the police officers got out. They locked the car with the boys inside, while one of the officers went to talk to a

Bangladeshi man. The man gave them some money. Zia looked out of the window and saw the logo of the petrol company Petronas. He was in Malaysia now.

7

MALAYSIA

Post-2012

Remembered from afar, Rakhine is golden. It shines in the Rohingya's poetry of the land, in memories of days spent in fields and forests or on the rivers that connect their village tracts. Rakhine's land, in their collective imagination, is not soaked in the blood of their children and parents. It is not scarred by the fires that incinerated their homes. Rakhine remains golden.

The Malaysia many Rohingya now inhabit is not golden, it is dull and suffocating. In just three years after the 2012 riots, until the trafficking camps were exposed, 170,000 Rohingya and Bangladeshis had been moved by sea. Far more had gone on the ships that left earlier, under the radar. The Rohingya did not find the freedom of fields and forests once they finally completed their journeys across seas and through the fingers of each hand that sold them to another. They found a Malaysia that is grey. It is the colour of a dream dulled by the reality of living on top of each other, in the forgotten tower blocks the twentieth century built for expanding cities, in boxes of aged concrete behind walls of flaking paint and plaster. Bangladesh's tarpaulin settlements may shake in the wind and bake under the sun, but they still offer a view of the Rakhine hills. The scent of the morning dew still sits on the air if you wander into nearby fields at sunrise.

Instead, they breathe Malaysian air that is heavy; it sits upon their shoulders inside homes that are little more than dark and humid bedrooms, barely larger than the mattress lying on the floor. Shared living rooms are made from a couple of square metres of carpet, a wall to lean on and a small kitchenette barely clinging to its hinges. The men flit in and out of these homes, between shifts on city jobs strange to them. The women sit inside, hidden behind locked doors and solid, wrought-iron security gates—they and the world locked away from each other. They cannot move as they do in villages or even in refugee camps, where although a woman or girl faces many dangers she can still mingle with her neighbours. The only human life a Rohingya woman in Malaysia might see during a normal day is that of her child or another Rohingya bride locked away in the same apartment. She may even hide from the tiny world inside— from the strange men she shares space with or even her own husband. When she talks, she says little. When visitors are around, her words come through her husband's mouth.

These husbands were not usually the men they arrived with. In some cases, the women were already married and followed young husbands who had taken the sea journey in earlier years. Others were like Asmida, sold into marriage by the traffickers. Many, however, were young women and girls scouted on behalf of young Rohingya men alienated from their own community and growing impatient. In the villages or refugee camps, their families would make enquiries among neighbours and relatives, visiting each other in the evenings to strike deals over tea and under tarpaulin, negotiating over dowries and who would pay the trafficking fees. They could be as eager for the marriage as the young man in Malaysia; a girl married off was one less mouth to feed and, anyway, neither Myanmar nor Bangladesh offered any girl much chance of an education or any other opportunity. She would then be sent onto those boats, to sit on the upper deck next to the captain's room. Later, she might talk about how other girls were taken into that room.

Sharifah

Sharifah Shakirah's nose wrinkles and her fists clench with all the concentrated frustration bottled inside her small frame whenever she thinks about these women, the ones she has not reached yet. She was not yet an adult when she began finding her way into their homes, trying to teach basic Malay and English to women older than herself because she wanted to share her one privilege—Sharifah had an education, of sorts.

She did not get it easily or conventionally. She had to start fighting for her education twenty years ago when she arrived in Malaysia as a child, to join a father she did not remember. He had been forced to run after he saw soldiers kill a group of Rohingya, executing some and burying the others alive, turning himself into a marked man. The family stayed behind, but for only as long as the calm lasted—which was not long at all. This was the early 1990s and Rakhine was becoming the tinder box that was sending its population into Bangladesh. Their neighbours were all Rakhine, and when the fires arrived in their village Sharifah's mother lost faith in their relationships lasting through what was to come. Instead of heading to Bangladesh, she decided to take the children to join their father.

But the journey would be long. They moved in darkness from their village to another, where they waited during the day for their chance to sneak into yet another village. There, at midnight, they boarded a boat filled with other Rohingya. The men were on the deck and the women, children and elderly huddled underneath. Sharifah could barely breathe. The faces all around her were tired, scared of the sounds of the water battering the boats and even more worried about the authorities who might stop them. Her mother hugged the children and prayed, and did both with even more zeal whenever they suspected a light shining in the distance might belong to the police. They spent those hours in silent fear until the boat reached its destination—the capital. From Yangon they were supposed to be forwarded to Malaysia, by land through Thailand, back at a time when that route was common for a variety of Burmese refugees looking for an escape from the margins elsewhere or the authorities chasing pro-democracy activists. It was not to be so straightforward. The traffickers locked the family into a shop and demanded a sum of money her mother could not afford. As the time allotted for their father to gather the money passed, Sharifah's mother grew nervous about being caught and decided she would pay for only the children to be released from the shop into the care of a relative. They escaped just in time but, just before her father was able to send the full amount for all of them to travel, Sharifah's mother was arrested and the children then split up among other relatives. The journey was off and Sharifah was sent to Mandalay.

There, she became a child servant. The family were distant relatives but they showed the young girl little sympathy, putting Sharifah to work cleaning, cooking and running errands. When they craved something to eat deep into the night, Sharifah was sent to the night market to cater to their fancies. When her father called, she was told to act normally and to ask him to send money for them. Depriving them of any of these demands would mean beatings. There was nowhere to go and no one to talk to. She was completely cut off from the world she knew. Instead of living in that golden Rakhine, Sharifah was stuck high in a concrete tower, in a room with no windows, where she knew only darkness and lost track of the day's hours. She found a friend in a dog that usually stood outside one of the houses she passed when running errands for the family.

"Whenever I passed on the road he would bark at me", she said. "So what I would do is I would go to him and talk to him for a few minutes and then I would laugh, then he would be quiet. So he became the only friend I had."

Her mother discovered what had been happening only when she was finally released her from prison after two years and deported to Rakhine. Getting out was going to be difficult, so the family began to round up the funds to send the children off to join their father, one by one. Sharifah was the last. She was taken by a female trafficker by car across the borders, first into Thailand and then towards those same jungles that merge into Malaysia, where two decades later camps would be built to house the numbers of Rohingya arriving there. A trafficker, the first person to show her any kindness since leaving Rakhine, held her hand as she crossed and pointed out her father, who sat waiting on a motorbike. It was the first time she could remember seeing him in person but she ran towards him, darting across the road without a thought to the passing traffic.

* * *

Sharifah became a refugee in a country where there are no refugees. There is no law to govern their existence and no paperwork issued by the Malaysian government to validate it. Malaysia, like Bangladesh, has never signed the 1951 Refugee Convention, though it has for decades absorbed people who fled conflict and autocracy elsewhere in Southeast Asia. This meant that Sharifah could not officially enrol in school. A local Malaysian school did, however, let her attend. She could sit in classes but not take exams. She could wear the uniform, but spent her days reminded by the other children that she was not one of them and mocked by the teacher for not knowing how to read at her age.

But Sharifah was strong-willed even as a child. The teacher's humiliation eventually only made her more determined to study and she took to storming into her mother's bedroom after school, locking her parents out on the other side of the door. Inside, Sharifah opened her books and stared at the English alphabet. She studied the shapes of the letters until she had memorised the sound each angle and curve was supposed to represent. Then she returned to school, proud.

"So you know the letters, at your age? These other children are all reading books", the teacher said.

The goalposts had been moved but Sharifah was by this point already galvanised by her adventure. She started to read the class's assigned books and by the end of the year had read them all, surpassing her classmates. When graduation came, Sharifah would have been on the stage with all others—had she been Malaysian. Instead, she stood at the back and watched them with the other girls in their dresses, collecting their certificates.

By her teens, having broken through the doors that schools had been slamming in her face, Sharifah decided to teach others. Her early arrival in Malaysia had been a blessing. With her father, she had at least been able to live as a child, not as a child forced to live with a strange man. So, when her father finished work every night, he took Sharifah around as she knocked on doors and sought out those other children, or grown women, who had not been granted the same opportunities as herself. He sat in the back as she tutored the girls in Malay and English from her own schoolbooks. Sharifah knew she was never going to be able to give them a full education and that these short lessons were not going to catapult the women to freedom, but she didn't expect perfection. It was enough to give them tools to live a little beyond the boxes they had been confined to in Malaysia.

By the time she was 16, Sharifah was well known for her work, even by some UN workers. They invited her to speak at a series of conferences, to talk about her life as a refugee. It was going to be the first time she would speak in English in public. It was a shock for both her and her family. Their lives had always been private. Sharifah's mother always had her children in her sight, forced to construct a protective bubble around them for preservation. After school, they came straight home. There was too much that could go wrong in even a moment of distraction. So, when a UN team came to take Sharifah to the event, her mother had a sudden panic about letting her young daughter go, to break their hiding and present herself to the public. It took 45 minutes to convince her, but eventually she relented. Sharifah's mother and father joined the conference themselves. They sat in the crowd without understanding the language Sharifah was speaking in, but listening proudly.

* * *

The sounds of a classroom, of words spoken in American-accented voices and echoed by tongues still wrapping themselves around the new sounds, emanate on the approach to the offices of the Rohingya Women's Development Network. It is a few small rooms, a few floors up inside an assuming tower block in a Kuala Lumpur suburb. The door sits behind iron gates in a grey, concreted corridor, but it opens up on a more colourful sight. Inside is the environment Sharifah has built. Rohingya children dart about while their mothers, freed for a few hours from their urban prisons, learn English and study their religion. Sharifah's office inside is simple—a desk of her own, a sofa and a table for the women to sit around—but it is a world beyond the iron gate for the women who come every day. When Sharifah sits with them, they beam. Everything is released as they talk to the woman who tells their husbands to take a back seat without blinking. Her confidence disarms many of the men, too, and she worries little about the others, though she is aware of the whispers among male Rohingya leaders who think calling her a feminist will intimidate her and keep others away. I visit Sharifah during my first trip to Malaysia, on the other side of the trafficking network. I have been trying to understand how Rohingya women live but found conversations guarded by men. Sharifah is different. The women around her are at ease and she has few reservations herself. Not long after we begin to talk, she launches into a long but lively monologue about everything that makes her angry. Even while she wins international plaudits and, much more importantly, the respect of the women who laugh and cry with her in this simple office, she has to tussle with men. Existing leaders tap into urban conservatism and religious interpretations paint Sharifah as some sort of troublemaker. "I'd really just like to punch them, you know?" she says.

On the days when they are not with her, the women have to contend with loneliness. They have come to Malaysia on danger-ous journeys to join their husbands and yet are haunted by the fear that they could lose those husbands forever, that their soli-tude would become permanent. Some, like Sayeeda, who has become Sharifah's close friend, have reason to fear being alone. She married to escape months of being stuck in a trafficker's *kampung* safe house on the border, where she saw men come and buy the young girls while others like her were left to be abused by traffickers. "The traffickers that kept me were always touching me", said Sayeeda. "As a Muslim, I didn't like this. I didn't want this happening to me all the time, so it was better for me to get married. Sometimes when we cried, they would pity us and leave us alone. Sometimes, they would do more and beat us. When a man was willing to marry me, I was freed from that." So, she fears the day her husband's phone might go dead. It happens to Rohingya women often, in times when seats turn cold in the cafes frequented by Rohingya men, where they gather around plates that remind them of home, on tables plastered with adverts for calling cards that allow them to ring Myanmar. The floor of Kuala Lumpur workshops and construction sites suddenly fall quiet. These are the signs that Malaysia's notorious immigration police have swept through. They know well where to find Malaysia's undocumented visitors, in the places where they work, meet and shop. Some get news of a raiding team's arrival beforehand and learn what the opportune times are to miss work. Others only understand what is happening when the uniforms descend on them, often too late to make a dash away from the construction site or through the back door. The UNHCR cards for which refugees struggle so hard mean nothing in the moment—almost everyone is taken to the station. The only way to avoid a spell in Malaysia's cramped and diseased detention centres, ruled by prison guards who wield bamboo canes, is with money. From the back of police vans, they are asked to get on the phones, to repeat a form of the phone call the traffickers forced them into for ransoms. If their friends cannot raise a few thousand ringgits as a bribe within a few hours, they are trucked off to prison.

It strikes terror through the Rohingya. Some try to save themselves by sleeping in the forests around Kuala Lumpur at night—in small makeshift tents hidden among bushes, built from a small, stilted platform and a tarpaulin cover. Others try desperately to leave the city, to find jobs on plantations or in the countryside where the roving eyes of the immigration police are less present.

Malaysia hosts hundreds of thousands of undocumented people. Some are refugees from the immediate neighbourhood: the Rohingya or others who came before, like the Vietnamese boat people of the 1970s and 1980s. Bangladeshi migrants and others from across Asia seek opportunity while Arabs fleeing protracted civil wars in Syria or Yemen, or political persecution elsewhere, take advantage of Malaysia's uniquely generous visa-free entries for Middle Eastern countries as a safer route to refuge than the boats to Europe. Many of these refugees and migrants are from Muslim-majority countries and see in Malaysia a "brotherly nation" that will take care of them. This was the Malaysia of Mahathirism, the image of a nation built under former Prime Minister Mahathir Mohamad, that was proud, independent, economically successful and not scared to identify the importance of Islamic values. Malaysia seemed like a sanctuary.

In reality, it was not. The lip service offered by Malaysian leaders grated against the way the country operated. The sort of tensions that lay beneath the surface in Malaysia, that once fuelled race riots, could still be turned against the country's many followers. Manual labour was often done by these undocumented foreigners but, despite the importance of this labour to Malaysia's functioning, their places of work were constantly raided. The worst outcome was to be sent to the overcrowded, disease-ridden detention centres where they are badly fed and their complaints are punished with the strike of a bamboo cane.

Zia had to learn to navigate this once he arrived in Malaysia. The police officers who had smuggled him into the country transferred him to a trafficker at a Petronas station in the north, who then passed him on to another. Altogether, he had been sold seven times since he was kidnapped in Bangladesh. He finally escaped when he and seven others were left alone with a single captor who fell asleep in his room. They barricaded the door from the outside, broke the window of their room and jumped out. They tried hailing cars but found most ignored them, apart from a trucker who Zia suspected was going to try and sell them on again—so when he stopped the truck, they ran again. They found a kindly Malaysian family, who became the first people to offer them help without being motivated by a desire for profit since Zia's brief rest at the mosque after escaping the UN shelter in Thailand. He stayed with them for a few days and was given food, water and finally a new pair of clothes. He washed the caked-on dirt from his body and used the family's phone to contact his mother. For the first time in several months he would speak to her freely, without the weight of a trafficker's ransom ruining their connection. He phoned his friends also and then took the family's suggestion that he travel southwards, to Johor Bahru, near Singapore. He found the type of work that most Rohingya do, in a restaurant where he was exploited, paid according to the whims of the owner and unable to complain because he had no legal right to stay in the country he had never chosen to come to.

Zia

The grouping of Southeast Asian countries known as ASEAN have rarely shown any sympathy for the Rohingya. They certainly do not go so far as to criticise Myanmar too heavily or to enact any kind of actual pressure on this member to change the policies that have forced the Rohingya out. That would be against their policy of non-intervention, even in the face of the most serious rights abuses. When the Rohingya were adrift on the Andaman Sea, cut off by the trafficking network that would shame several of these ASEAN nations, they finally treated it as a crisis. It was a crisis they tried to limit by towing boats back to sea, but they would never redirect the conversation back onto the causes. Instead, they focused on the Bangladeshis on the boats, demonised them as illegal immigrants who had latched on to the desperate Rohingya as a way to secure riches. Malaysia, though it also towed boats out to sea, spoke the most strongly of ASEAN nations about the Rohingya, in the sympathetic terms that Muslim nations must always echo about "brotherly nations". Later, in 2017, it finally criticised Myanmar.

In this environment, Zia found a voice. Unlike in Bangladesh, speaking out here did not mean a visit from intelligence when the foreign visitors had completed their momentary glance at the camps, returning them to being unseen. Rohingya like Zia or Sharifah were now invited to conferences, to speak in English to gatherings of NGO workers, rights activists, philanthropists and politicians who saw some currency in speaking a sentence in favour of the Rohingya. The Malaysian Prime Minister Najib Razak even visited some of these conferences, giving Zia the chance to advocate directly to the most powerful man in the country: a man with the power to ease their suffering in exile— and maybe even at home. Zia was even able to snap a selfie with Najib. On Facebook, the reaction was wild, filling his contemporaries with admiration. A Malaysian filmmaker even turned that moment into a film about Zia's journey to Malaysia.

But it was all a false promise. The boats were still towed out to sea, and Malaysia and ASEAN took no action against Myanmar. Malaysia never moved any closer to recognising refugees and the immigration police did not stop their raids. A generation of Rohingya children born in Malaysia have no better prospect of education than their parents did before they jumped on boats. For all the glamour of meeting a prime minister, Zia still finds himself writing letters to UNHCR for Rohingya who have spent years inside the country without being registered for a card, leaving them vulnerable. In Kuala Lumpur cafes, he is introduced to Rohingya as someone who can help. Some are those he knew in his previous life, who had escaped or been expelled from Bangladesh. He shared the strongest connection with them—with people like Abdul Goni, who had not chosen Malaysia but had been stolen away from his family when he went out in search of a way to support them. Zia knew the grandmother who had raised Abdul Goni through a rough childhood, where his love for martial arts had been the brightness in his life and the thing everyone else knew him for. On his phone he swipes through a few photos that have been saved of that past, his knees bent and his fist extended in a Bruce Lee-style stance. Now Abdul Goni lives a sad life and when they sit together in a Kuala Lumpur McDonald's, he demonstrates how he works in a factory with one eye on the door, ready to duck at the sight of a police officer.

These men whom Zia meets like this, the ones he knows and the ones he does not, show him the letters they send monthly to UNHCR and the old papers they have from another time—UNHCR cards from Bangladesh that have no value in Malaysia or one of the various identity cards Myanmar cycled through for the Rohingya, none of which offered security and certainly not citizenship. Each of them had ultimately ended up at a very similar destination, regardless of what route they had taken. Zia's long journey and the experience of being sold like a fish plucked from water and sent through a supply chain had made it all click into place—there was nowhere to go. They were stateless in Myanmar, but they were also stateless everywhere, finding Bangladesh or Malaysia spared them murder but did not offer freedom. Some of the men Zia now sat with and tried to help could not remember Myanmar at all, like himself and some others who had never seen it. Others had grown up there, fleeing at some point to Bangladesh or getting straight on the boats from the Bay of Bengal. The injustice began to itch on Zia's skin. Resettlement was the one hope for peace, and it was granted to almost no one. Here, in this concrete jungle that had been spoken of as a utopia for persecuted Muslims, Zia saw the bigger picture. He started to write a book, realising his story had now bisected with so many of his compatriots—those he grew up with, who shared space on boats and in jungles, and now the ones who simply existed, in a large but loose community that was constantly frightened.

The family Zia had left behind in Bangladesh comprised not only his mother and her relatives. Though still young and not particularly keen on the idea, he had been given an arranged marriage. There was no particular emotion in it for either of them at the time, just the knowledge that it was routine and, expected of them—the fate of a young Rohingya boy and girl raised in tents. Anyway, in the camps there was little other purpose they could give to their lives than building a family and ensuring the Rohingya nation survived, even if in exile and destitution. That family were in the process of being formed when Zia was snatched away from them, his first daughter born while he was on his long journey. When he was finally settled in Johor Bahru, he tried to send some money back home though he was not keen on his wife taking the journey he had, to risk her and the child falling into the hands of predatory traffickers. But her family were keen and they organised her trip without talking to him, sending her on the boats to Malaysia along with their daughter. It was not a trip without risks, but compared with Zia's and with guarantors willing to pay the money it went more smoothly. She and Zia eventually settled in Kuala Lumpur. A couple of years passed in this new country, and he was more settled and established. He became involved in the activist community and earned a little more money as a translator, even if that work was sporadic. So, they settled in a flat in a northern suburb of the city. It was up a few flights of stairs and behind an iron gate that secured the door—small but clean and comfortable enough. It was not shared with strange people and the area was not so full of Rohingya and other migrants that it was constantly under the eye of the authorities. It was safe enough. Inside those rooms, Zia began to work on writing his story. He wanted to tell the world what had happened to him and his people.

* * *

If there is one place where the Rohingya can live in a shared space, it is online. Rivers and seas are bridged, checkpoints disappear and travel permits become irrelevant on Facebook, where the Rohingya preface their names with "Ro" to repurpose traditional Burmese title customs. They write poems that hark back to their golden Rakhine—a land some of them have never felt under their feet—and in the comments sections they congregate. Many of these friendships are purely virtual, connections made around debates or, more commonly, a collective cheer for a rousing post about their land or culture or how they should fight the helplessness that constantly haunts them. Zia opens the app on his phone to connect with the friends he was stripped from, to celebrate their weddings and the births of their children. It is also how a young Rohingya can die in Sri Lanka and be mourned by Zia in Malaysia, their old friends in Bangladesh and his brother in Ireland.

But the minds of young Rohingya glued to their phones are no less immune than any other youths' to the longing social media inspires. While the aspirational Rohingya of the Bangladeshi refugee camps post selfies on Kutupalong's hills or with young children playing, depending on the season, in the dust or the mud, on social media they are taunted by glimpses of where they want to be. Their friends who have escaped post selfies in luxurious cafes, on green cricket fields, from places where they can study and work, and with prime ministers. They stand on stages and speak to crowds who want to listen to the Rohingya. Stuck with frustrated ambitions, each photo fuels a desire to move beyond the camp's dust.

"They see my selfie with the prime minister and they think there's something here worth coming for, but I wish I could be back there with my family", said Zia. "That's my home."

The selfies are incomplete. They show the highlights, moments in front of tall and shiny buildings like the Petronas Towers where Rohingya occasionally wander, but never from the places they work and hide. Zia's most famous selfie, with Najib, was the same. It was his pride, a symbol of his successes, but as time passed he realised those moments meant little to the people in power. They posed with refugees and paid lip service to their causes but did little more. Zia also began to worry it gave off an image of success and freedom that was encouraging friends to follow him to Malaysia, where they thought he was proof that their wasted talents would finally find some use. Their arrivals were often not immediately known to him. He stumbled across them in different corners of the capital or on trips through the country, familiar faces spotted in small restaurants or cafes known to friends staying locally.

Some lived in quieter cities and towns that were like sanctuaries, a long way from the capital, where they lived with relative freedom and faced less hostility from locals. Others barely strayed beyond the northern towns where they were dropped off on the way down from Thailand. For some this might mean a quiet life, but the more aspirational knew the best they could do would be to find a small job teaching or translating for an NGO: nothing more than a meagre wage to pay their rent and send a little home, enough to survive but do little more.

One of those places was Alor Setar, a sleepy city that served as the state capital of Kedah, on the border with Thailand and a short ferry ride from Langkawi, the island geared towards tourists but which had often seen Rohingya boats turn up unannounced on its beaches. Zia and I left for the city on an early flight from Kuala Lumpur. We met in the centre of the capital and took a taxi that gave us another chance to talk about all that he remembered from Bangladesh and everything he missed— mostly the mother he only saw through pixellated video calls and asked me to visit whenever I was in Bangladesh. Zia's UNHCR card allowed him to take domestic flights within Malaysia, but he and most Rohingya still rarely used that option and, besides the cost of flying, it became obvious why when we tried to pass through security. We had to show boarding passes, which were not a problem, and either a passport or valid form of identity. For the first, second and third airport officials who stopped us, Zia's UNHCR card was not enough to board a plane—he had to have a passport, they insisted. If he had not travelled by plane, for the first time, a month earlier, accompanying an NGO worker, he might have given up. But he knew he had the right to travel and stood his ground, forcing the officials to shuttle back and forth until they reached a senior who accepted Zia's card.

The journey itself was straightforward and we were met in Alor Setar by Rofique, a friend of Zia's who taught at a refugee school in the city. Rofique had come straight from Myanmar as a young teen who was incredibly talented at school, but had to work in Malaysia in a way that made no use of or developed his skills. He went through the usual cycle of labouring while trying to continue to educate himself, before finding simple roles that gave him a little more purpose. He and Zia had not known each other before Malaysia but their drive to help the other Rohingya around them brought them together. He took us first to meet a group of Rohingya families crammed into three small rooms above factories and workshops in an industrial park. There were no iron cages blocking their room doors, as in Kuala Lumpur, but the building itself was far worse, made of flimsy material never meant for housing and decaying floor tiles. The men worked in plantations just outside of the city and the women stayed locked inside, offered little by this small town where they were obviously outsiders. As usual, they did what they could to stay beyond the watch of the authorities. Some of their children stayed at a madrassa on the city's edge, studying the Qur'an in a single room where a couple of dozen small children sat on hard floors rocking back and forth to the rhythm of the passages they recited. It was no formal education, but the families valued the knowledge.

Later, we went to meet up with some of Zia's other friends in a small *kampung*-style house in a quiet part of the city. Though still tired, with its paint peeling in the humidity that had the children splayed out on a mattress in the corner, it felt more like a home than many Rohingya abodes in Malaysia. The alleys outside were quiet, village-like, and several other Rohingya lived nearby. On a large square cloth spread across the floor was an array of Rohingya dishes—the necessary bowl of rice, a chicken curry and a mash of chillies and onions that accompanied most meals. Zia and Rofique finally caught up after a day showing me around, but they also introduced me to someone whom I had wanted to meet: one of the newer arrivals from Bangladesh. His name was Imran, wellknown to many of those I knew in Bangladesh. He had for years been an elected camp leader in Kutupalong and had spent his life tussling with the camps for dignity, for himself and his neighbours. He was stockier than most Rohingya, having spent his time in offices and meetings earning money through aid and advocacy rather than labour, and spoke English with fluency and flourish. He had spent his entire life in Kutupalong, helping the batch of new arrivals who fled Rakhine in October 2016, but soon afterwards decided he wanted something more. The constant struggle for a more stable existence in Bangladesh had achieved little, and he knew Myanmar offered no future anytime soon. He had seen it himself during a few weeks back in his home village in Rakhine, where he had smuggled himself to see family members he had never known, but learned what it meant to be in constant fear of the Tatmadaw. The October arrivals had only confirmed how far off a Rohingya return was. So, he came to Malaysia, the land where he had seen his old friend Zia shaking hands with prime ministers and friends posing under the lights of Kuala Lumpur's twin towers. He hoped a mind sharpened from solving community-based problems within the camp setting might find a platform like Zia's, to talk about the Rohingya in a major international capital rather than in a forgotten corner of Bangladesh. In reality, Kuala Lumpur was distant and unreasonable, too difficult to live in without steady work for a newcomer and the actual opportunities to speak up were far too rare for all those who wanted to speak up. Alor Setar was a backwater where he only ever felt frustrated.

"I don't see any difference between Bangladesh and Malaysia", he said. "The life I lived in Bangladesh is a refugee life and the life I live in Malaysia is a refugee life. You don't have any facilities, you're not allowed to live. You can have the UNHCR card, but you cannot work. I feel frustrated, I feel hopeless. This is not a life, this is just survival."

* * *

In their usual spots in cafes and canteens, the Rohingya men of Malaysia spent the last days of August 2017 glued to their phones, swiping, typing and constantly hoping the next alert would bring new information from Rakhine. Not knowing what was happening to their families was again feeding the fear and guilt that had tormented them during the 2012 riots and the Tatmadaw's operation the previous October. They had no border to rush to. There was no physical act they could perform to help their people, and even communicating with their families was impossible with everyone on the run or in hiding. Their budget smartphones were the only window into what was happening, the pings from WhatsApp a warning of violent images that filled all with anger and some with hate, even vengeance. They had not seen their mothers since they were young teenagers sent on missions to earn for their families, into an exile based on sacrifice. Now they searched for the features of their mothers in the faces of the women arriving on the Bangladeshi border. It made them wish they were back in Rakhine, that they were standing against this military that had only ever made them suffer. It made many wish they were fighting. Others were more practical. Though all they had ever received from Malaysia's leaders were words of sympathy, the more action-minded were ready to push the boundaries of the freedom and connections they had negotiated in Malaysia. If they could not be on the frontline, saving lives, then they could be the megaphone. Zia was not just glued to his phone absorbing the traumatic material coming through, he repackaged it for other audiences in social media and spoke on online panels quickly set up in reaction. When there were protests outside embassies, Zia went to show the cameras that the Rohingya existed. All of the images, reports and rumours that flew around Rohingya social media networks started to be filtered by the Rohingya media groups established in Malaysia. Some were just individuals operating with a phone and their contacts, but others were trying to build more. R Vision was a TV channel that lived online, operating from a crowded building block around the corner from one of Kuala Lumpur's typical suburban malls. Shoes off, R Vision's reporters all sat by a dozen desks, busy verifying reports to write up on their website and social media. They processed the first images of gunfire crackling around the twenty-five villages that were first attacked in August and later that day the first people fleeing Tong Bazar. They had videos of Chilhali village in Rathedaung blanketed in dark smoke and of its survivors setting up shelters for the night alongside concealed paths they were hacking from the forested hills. They collected footage from massacre sites like Tula Toli as it emerged from the survivors arriving in Bangladesh, publishing it without comment to create an archive on their social media timelines of the massacres. A few presenters rotated between a single seat set against a green wall and facing a camera that recorded their daily news bulletins in Rohingya, Burmese and English. These were the Rohingya who dared to live openly. Their language skills and education had meant they could connect with people of influence in Malaysia and further abroad, giving them a measure of protection unlike the other refugees who went missing without being noticed beyond their community. They were now determined to use that privilege at a time when their people needed their skills the most, for the world was now starting to pay attention. R Vision's founder Mohammad Noor was aware of this and, from his office adjoining the busy newsroom, he thought up big-idea projects that might finally take off, around standardising Rohingya scripts that had been in development for decades or securing access to finance and identity documents that would allow them to live normally. This Malaysia-based activist community, which had been so frustrated for so long, suddenly saw a bit of progress. While Myanmar tried to frame the narrative of the massacres into a global war-on-terror framework, Malaysia finally exerted its unique position to speak more bluntly to Myanmar. Bangladesh had also decided to become more vocal, but Malaysia breaking ASEAN's code of silence was more powerful. When its leaders accused Myanmar of war crimes it was newsworthy across the region. It also had standing in the Muslim world and its positions became talking points that meant the Rohingya's name was for the first time properly heard in the Arab world, making headlines on every satellite news channel and spoken on Fridays in the prayers of the imams at Jerusalem's Al-Aqsa mosque alongside their own struggle as Palestinians. Suddenly, everyone knew who the Rohingya were and it seemed the world was ready to talk about them.

* * *

The Rohingya did not stop walking once they arrived in Bangladesh. They came in from the east, set their tents and then were forced to start shuttling further westwards, on a daily journey doomed to only ever get longer. Their lives were saved by this new home on the hills, but it had been made with no planning. Hastily hewn from the existing landscape, Kutupalong was cumbersome and devoid of necessities. They drilled for water and often found nothing. They were given food but no fuel to cook it with or to warm themselves through the coming winters. The returning refugees remembered how deceptively cold they would be, the humidity helping the chill reach deeper inside their chests even when a thermometer suggested moderate temperatures. So, instead of recuperating they began walking again, trudging off in search of firewood. They left after prayers at dawn, hoping to get back before the sun beat too heavily on their tired backs, where scars soon began to develop from sharp branches rubbing against the skin. Quickly, well-trodden paths were snaking out of the camps and into a forest that seemed to be in retreat. Along these routes were refugees rushing out or returning, slumped under the weight of firewood hauls as big as any of them could carry. On the sides, they stopped for short breaks and the most tired, often small children sent out by families missing the young men usually assigned these tasks, tore roots from trees already harvested by the more able. The thirsty drank straight from murky puddles left by recent storms.

This was the camp settling. By December 2017, life was beginning to take form. It was not made for Momtaz, though there were many like her. She had to rely on the charity of neighbours, unable to make such strenuous journeys with her injuries and unwilling to send her only remaining child on such a mission. Other women and their children had to venture out alone into these ungoverned forests, braving the threats of wild animals, predatory men and locals both angry at their disappearing forest and seeking to profit from the new arrivals. The number of those still arriving had slowed. The transit camps were more able to handle the transition and had fewer injured to deal with. The UN was now thinking less about how to facilitate the safety of people from Myanmar, but were bringing 100,000 or so Rohingya who had settled in the Chittagong Hill Tracts, where a smaller number of Rohingya who lived furthest north in Rakhine State had sought the most immediate escape route. The decision had been made that the Cox's Bazar camps would be the holding place for all Rohingya. This settled version of the camp, a hasty annex that now dwarfed the original settlement, did not appear to be a place to build a future—without fuel or water and not a single place to hide from the cyclones and monsoon seasons that humanitarians already had to start thinking about. Bangladesh was already talking about repatriations, ready to turn back the generosity that had encouraged self-congratulation and talk inside the country of a Nobel Peace Prize for Sheikh Hasina. It banned SIM cards and set up checkpoints between the camps, the first measures to ensure the Rohingya did not feel comfortable. Yet despite this, it was becoming a home of sorts, a place where broken families were gradually reunited whether they had been fractured during their recent escape or decades earlier. The feeling of homelessness that had seized Rohingya abroad motivated them to seek long-lost families. The homeless, untethered Rohingya abroad sought ways back to their people. The privileged few who had been resettled in rich countries arrived with aid while the lonely boys of Malaysia, broken by the powerlessness they had felt during August and September, had already found ways to join their families in Bangladesh. They could once again return to their mothers' arms and eat breakfasts with their families.

But there were also returns from less obvious places, where the Rohingya had been staying without so much attention and whose returns were less voluntary. The shock of that summer's violence was not enough to save them from hosts losing patience. These other returnees began trickling into Bangladesh, slipping into this camp superstructure so big it could never account for everyone. They came from Saudi Arabia, where the state's restructuring under Crown Prince Mohammed bin Salman had led to undocumented workers being detained en masse. The

Rohingya were not spared the fate of the Shumaysi detention centre, a sterile facility on the road between Mecca and Jeddah where the migrants, stacked on metal bunk beds, rarely felt any light that was not artificial or breeze not recycled through air conditioning units. Their only escape from this indefinite detention was to find a way to buy papers to secure deportation to Bangladesh, a process that involved being bussed to the airport in handcuffs and locked in isolated waiting rooms, only to risk being arrested in Bangladesh for holding falsified documents.

At the same time, others arrived in Bangladesh from India, where Narendra Modi's ruling Hindu nationalist Bharatiya Janata Party was not hesitant in agitating against them as part of a Muslim conspiracy against Hinduism—an echo of the threat that Myanmar posited the Rohingya posed to Buddhism. When there were arson attacks on the slums where Rohingya lived in Jammu and Delhi, no action was taken even when their activists proudly claimed responsibility for them. The balance of fear tipped when the government deported a small group to Myanmar and soon afterwards began a drive to register the refugees, requiring fingerprints and eye scans and asking them to fill in unfamiliar forms with Burmese writing. They feared it was a way to trick them into returning to Myanmar.

It had been more than a year since Momtaz, discharged from the hospital on a stormy night, had first set eyes on the new Kutupalong being forged, but here there were still more Rohingya staring upon it with fresh eyes—from Myanmar, Malaysia, India and Saudi Arabia. It was by now almost fully formed, though it continued to grow and change—more sophisticated as it was adapted to host them, but also more complicated as needs deferred on arrival became more urgent over time. This was not just a place they had come for their survival, for respite; Kutupalong had become the place where the Rohingya existed as a nation. Myanmar had shunted them across the border and now other countries were doing the same.

PART 3

8

THE WORLD'S LARGEST CAMP

Momtaz (March 2018)

Propped up against her shelter's bamboo doorway, Momtaz sorts through a pile of cellophane-wrapped clothing and hands them over for inspection to her guests—a couple of Bangladeshi women dressed in *salwar kameez*, concealing their faces behind a stretch of their headscarves pinned by the ear. They nod their approval, quickly haggle a price and hand Momtaz 100 taka for the three items. Then they leave her shelter to see which of her neighbours might have another deal for them. Friday afternoons, after the weekly prayer, bring many of these women to the camps when the never-ending infrastructure works are paused and aid operations take a day off. The relative calm permits door-to-door shopping trips in search of whatever the refugees can offer. Clothing, soap, food and household items are all available far below the market price. Those same items in the local markets that Bangladeshi women would usually attend have been inflated since aid groups flooded in to buy up stock wholesale—some of it ending up back in the shops with new branding—and they can no longer afford the basics. The dresses Momtaz has just earned a dollar on were handed to her at the aid centre a day earlier but were a Bengali style of clothing she is not comfortable wearing, so she decided they would be more useful converted into a little change. The money is not going to buy her any luxuries, but it does offer a little flexibility that she is desperate for—the limited rations she received cannot pay for the medical treatment she and Rozeya need. Since her life was saved, Momtaz has received no dedicated secondary care. Six months have passed and her nights are still restless, still wracked with mental anguish. Her head physically hurts and her skin itches. The local clinics in Balukhali offer nothing but some kind of syrup-based children's painkiller that does nothing for her. Not a single dedicated facility in the camp offers serious pain management, baulking at the idea of offering stronger painkillers like morphine despite the lifelong injuries people are now living with. The only decent treatment is at the MSF hospitals, but both the original hospital near Kutupalong market and a new facility built on the hills further inside the camp are inaccessible to Momtaz. They would take a few hours to walk to and she would have to drag Rozeya there. Alternatively, she would have to cough up money for transport. Everything boils down to money. Momtaz needs it for medicine, for fuel, for any nutrition not provided by lentils and simply to visit her sister Dildar, who lives over on the other hills. Men can earn wages, albeit meagre, working on camp infrastructure projects or in fields and factories nearby but there are few opportunities for women and almost nothing for Momtaz, frail and alone.

"I have no money and if I ever have a little bit, it goes so quickly", she says. "There's nothing to eat, nothing for us to make do with. I sell these clothes because I have nothing else to sell, just some lentils and rice that I need. Some money comes in and straight away it goes to the doctor."

Her voice has healed in the months that have passed, but it still croaks and she still strokes a bored Rozeya's hair where the long machete scar is now slightly more hidden behind the tufts of hair trying to reclaim their place. They have tried to heal and, physically, they have managed to a little, but Momtaz cannot escape how much her life has changed and spends her long, lonely hours ruminating over everything that she has lost. "I spend every day trying to figure out my life, thinking about my family, my villagers", she says. "I don't have anything for me, everyone was killed there. I survived but why was it me who came here?"

Only months have passed since August's great upheaval and the relief of reprieve is already rapidly fading. Momtaz and her neighbours had never thought of complaining about any of the camp's hardships when they first arrived. At least they were safe and had some form of shelter. But the camp seemed weighed down by fatigue from their inescapably dreary existence. As a Rohingya woman, alone in Bangladesh, Momtaz has to fend for herself in a hostile environment. Her family, which had once lived in a single village, were now fractured atop many hills, each one strange to them. There are no lights at night, so going to the toilet is a frightening prospect in a world full of men she does not know, who escape crimes by disappearing into the crowds without facing even the most basic justice. The toilets and bathing spaces are all shared and labelled in languages not understood. An M for Male identifies some facilities, but is often taken for *mohilla*—woman. There is a certain safety in your own block but, to venture beyond, women pull veils over their faces for security as much as faith, to attempt to blend into a crowd of women, to avoid the lingering gazes of men. Some of the widows of Rakhine live in a sort of commune, guarded against the outside. Others like Momtaz cradle their children at night, alone, tortured by stories of tarpaulin walls breached by a criminal's blade, terrified when occasionally a mosque's loudspeaker blares an alert that a child has been snatched. There is no path towards justice in these cases. Complaints are at the mercy of the *majhi* or the *shomaj*, committees of elders who decide whether the complaints should be passed on to the Camp in Charge (CiC), the individual official who is the law of his camp. Stolen children disappear and abused women and girls end up forced into silence.

There was little in the way of educational or work opportunities in Rakhine, but this new threat for young Rohingya girls is even more constant than that of the marauding Burmese soldiers. Families do not want their girls out under the gaze of others: washing their clothes, collecting water, going to the toilet—everything is too public, too dangerous. Rohingya brides are often young anyway, but early marriage is increasingly seen by parents as their solution to the social problems they fear the camps are breeding, as a way to pass a girl on into the protection of another man with the added benefit of her food becoming his responsibility, as though a burden transferred.

After the two Bangladeshi women leave Momtaz's shelter, her aunt—the same one who had recognised her bandaged body on the day she found her way back to their corner of Balukhali—asks if Momtaz has got married recently. She has heard that she had. The question immediately sets Momtaz on edge and her first instinct is to deny it. It is almost unthinkable, she tells her aunt, for her to be married. To make the point she strokes her face and leg to emphasise the scars along her body: "Look at these, who would marry me?" They both sit quietly for a moment and then Momtaz relents. She actually has married, out of necessity. He is young and healthy, so although he does not live with her and is not around much—he already has another wife—the arrangement offers her some protection and perhaps some help with this refugee life. There are moments when it has given her some reason to be positive, that something good has changed in her life, but she also feels guilt, consumed by the constant thoughts of her slaughtered family and the question of why only she and Rozeya survived. This marriage is not to be celebrated, she says aloud, as if she has to justify it, it is just a way to stumble through the difficulties this new life keeps throwing at her.

The man abandoned her after a few weeks. It was all too easy for a man to disappear from a wife in the mass of the camps, to find a new wife and home somewhere it would be difficult to be traced. It had been happening for thirty years and is only easier now the camps are so large. Evidence is only anecdotal, and the prevalence exaggerated by local Bangladeshis quick to accept negative stereotypes of the refugees, even though Bangladeshi men have married Rohingya women, only to do the same. A fear of crime, drug-taking and alcohol use has also grown among the new refugees, traits they associated with the trapped Rohingya youth of previous refugee generations. They fear their own youth will start to fall into this same trap, in marriages between young people burdened by unhandled trauma, in an environment where destructive habits might fill the gaps left by lack of opportunity, freedom or even the mundane ways of survival that characterised life in between the military's attacks in Rakhine. This was enough to make young Rohingya girls wary of marrying their male counterparts in the camps—to the benefit of the legion of bachelors in Malaysia, some of whom had taken the perilous trips there precisely because they saw it as the only way to make a life suitable for marriage. This was also how the traffickers found their way back into the camps.

* * *

The demand to move people, some of their own will and others to fill appetites for cheap or forced labour, has always existed in Bangladesh—the land of the *dalaal*. The predators were primed even in the first days after August 2017, sensing opportunity to profit from the worst type of human crisis. They snatched young women as they crossed into the strange new country, often unaccompanied by families who sent them ahead because of the rampaging soldiers' reputation for rape, unaware of similar threats awaiting on the other side. They posed as rescuers offering to guide the women to the camps, but drove them to far more distant places. Some were caught in Chittagong—eight hours away—on traffic stops when police suspicions were raised because the women could not answer questions about where they were going. An unknown number of women were trafficked undetected, delivered to brothels as far as India, or more commonly into domestic work in cities. Aspiring *dalaals* with the right links found it easy to recruit domestic workers, targeting the children of single mothers who struggled to buy even the bamboo they needed to build their homes. The new humanitarian presence that soon rushed in helped temporarily to quell some of this early chaos. The provision of shelter and food made life feel less desperate, but the earliest arrivals had to scramble for themselves with whatever money they had brought with them or begged for beside the road.

And yet the trafficking network still fought to stay relevant. In Thailand, the trafficking camps had been shut down since 2015 and would not be easily reopened—but the network itself was not dead, only dormant. There were still boats waiting on the Bangladeshi coast. There were still safe houses for their prospective passengers and cars ferrying them between the refugee camps and the same old launching points. They had never gone away, even though the Bangladeshi police and coastguard had shut down activity at sea in a way they had never done before. Now there were also eyes on Cox's Bazar, with Bangladeshi police informing the local media of each success in stifling the traffickers—whether it was stopping the transfer of passengers on the road, busting down safe-house doors or catching boats trying to sneak off into the Bay of Bengal after dark. Their numbers were still small but the traffickers attempted to test the waters, to see how many they could recruit and how freely they could move people. They knew that cracks would eventually emerge; that the authorities would not be incorruptible; and that, as life continued, basic rations and the simplest of existences could not satisfy the Rohingya's family and cultural demands forever.

It was through Sharifah that I first heard of the young women already arriving in Malaysia in the first few months of 2018. Young men in Malaysia had started to contact their parents or used their friends as ways to find brides, which was easy when they could reel off Malaysia's false promises of an escape from an existence that was already becoming obviously harder. On arrival, they are referred to Sharifah to help in settling into the new country. Some of the first arrived from Sittwe on small boats that managed to directly reach the Malaysian coast undetected. Sharifah is able to talk to some of them, but other women who want to meet her are blocked by brothers or husbands who do not want Sharifah's involvement. The more she speaks to them, the more she realises that most are no longer coming by sea but through other routes less scrutinised by the authorities. A very small number come by air with falsified Bangladeshi passports, but this method is expensive and Bangladeshi authorities are actively working to catch out Rohingya who try to beat the system. Far more arrive by land, using old routes like the one Sharifah herself arrived on, but which were forgotten over the years when sea travel could so easily transport thousands more.

Back in Bangladesh, it does not take much to find families who had sent or were considering sending their daughters. On Sharifah's suggestion, Yassin and I ask around and manage to speak to half a dozen families within a few hours, some who he personally knows and others who simply come up in conversation and are pointed out by their neighbours. Our first stop is Hamida, a family friend from Yassin's village who he calls his aunt. She has recently seen first-hand how it all worked. Her son arranged his own marriage to a girl who was still living in Rakhine, after she had been unable to help find a bride for him. The act of getting the girls to Malaysia became part of their transnational marriage negotiations, conducted over phones and social media apps rather than under each other's hospitality in their own homes. Typical to many cultures in the region, dowries were usually paid to the husband, but now these prices were often waived by the frustrated young men in Malaysia who were also willing to pay some of the trafficking costs and sometimes all. They had been away from home too long and saw no other way of visiting their people or marrying within Malaysia—the customs were not that important.

The 15-year-old daughter-in-law was first smuggled into Bangladesh to spend a week living with Hamida, who got to know and like the young girl so much her departure was difficult. Hamida had no idea it would take two months. But the girl's journey fit the general pattern almost exactly. Though many girls came from Myanmar, they still had to get into Bangladesh so they could be driven from the camps to re-enter Myanmar further north. They were never told they were re-entering the country, but it was geographically impossible to not do so. Essentially blindfolded by their lack of knowledge, the traffickers led them on the journey, skirting the parts of Rakhine where it was too easy to be caught moving as a Rohingya. They crossed borders, scaled hills, went through jungles and waded across waterways. Sometimes they stopped and waited, they changed cars or made some of the journey on foot or by boat. The girls were not told why things happened or where they were but, somehow, this journey snaked through Myanmar's peripheral states into southern Thailand and then, finally, over that porous jungle border into Malaysia. There were no weeks spent at sea or in trafficking camps but it was still a month or two for young girls left at the will of traffickers, completely cut off from contact despite their parents justifying their early marriages in the name of protecting them from predators. In Thailand, Hajj Ismail was getting similar calls to Sharifah, from authorities who needed assistance with the groups being intercepted near the southern forests. They were being caught at safe houses when neighbours complained, alerted by the smells that emanated from the safe houses after months without bathing. Hajj Ismail travelled himself from Bangkok to the detention centre and found, sitting on hard floors of a holding facility, dozens of tired, weak young people—most of them in their mid-teens, most of them girls.

Back in Cox's Bazar, Hamida knows another family in her camp who are thinking about sending their own daughter. They live a few minutes away, in a cluster of shelters pinned to the top of a clay hill. Their neighbours are blaring Bengali pop music through a small speaker connected to a phone and we ask where to find the family, who are in the last of a row of shelters. They are all inside, not doing much, and they agree to talk, handing us short stools to sit on by the doorway while they sit inside, out of view. Though this land journey was forgotten for so long, the stories of its hardships are starting to be remembered as accounts are passed back to families by the girls who have already arrived. So this family have an idea of how long it could take, how exposed their daughter would be, and yet they are still considering sending her. The mother, Khaleda, thinks marriage abroad offers her daughter protection from the evils of a refugee camp. Even schools, she says, take girls out of the watchful eye and into danger without offering any benefit that could change their lives in the camps. An offer had come in from Malaysia but the man was not offering to pay the trafficking fees and they cannot afford it themselves, so they still view marriage within the camps as a possibility unless they find some means of financing the journey. Whatever happens, marriage is inevitable. The girl does not reveal herself as we speak. She sits in the corner, in the shadows, listening to her parents' answers. Eventually, she offers a few of her own words and admits she is not keen on the idea. She cannot imagine leaving her parents to live somewhere else, let alone another country where she might face the prospect of never seeing them again. But she will do whatever her family tell her to do.

9

REORGANISING

August 2018

On a set of hills facing Rakhine, a few thousand Rohingya boys sit down in white shirts and dark green *longyis*—the typical uniform of a school in Myanmar. Dawn has just risen on 25 August, a year since the Tatmadaw's operations, and this is their way of showing they still exist and intend to return, with rights. There are other, older demonstrators with them on those hills and there are leaders who have stood up to deliver speeches thanking Bangladesh and damning Myanmar. They have spoken about justice and citizenship and have rejected Myanmar's derogatory offers of being registered as foreign residents under the NVC system, mocking the government's claim that it is a pathway to citizenship. They know better. Elsewhere, groups rally on the roads and a squadron of women draped in black hold their own protest. It is more forceful and filled with more pain, demanding justice for the very specific crimes they had been subjected to. The Rohingya are announcing their civil society in exile. It has been forged in a year that has passed rapidly, each month bringing some panic that has shaken the refugees enough to remind them that safety is not guaranteed. There are concerns about healthcare, over fires that ripped through markets and about confused elephants rampaging through shelters that have encroached on their traditional migratory paths. With Bangladesh's national election coming up, the roads are still decorated in banners declaring Sheikh Hasina the "Mother of Humanity"—the name bestowed on her by her own party for opening the borders—but Bangladesh has become decidedly less welcoming. It has begun to push a rotation of threats about starting repatriations or relocating the refugees to Bhasan Char, a remote island in the Bay of Bengal formed from transitory deposits of silt. Fears about the "disaster within a disaster" if a cyclone should hit the camps have luckily not been realised, but the monsoon rains have still broken shelters and caused landslides on hills that lost their structural integrity when they were stripped of the trees that held them together.

Mere survival is not going to define the Rohingya. This first year has taught them what it would mean to be known as refugees. Their lives have become known as a crisis, photographed and written about, made the subject of films—all of which have won awards for their creators. Some of the most traumatised victims were shown to visiting diplomats and major celebrities draped in UN logos and followed by cameras. The refugees believed these people who borrowed their trauma had the power to solve something, that they had the power to return them and had not acted before only because they were unaware that genocide loomed. But as more people came to talk and the others never returned once their selfie had been posted, the Rohingya grew weary. The young male translators realised they were processing the same words repeatedly without purpose. Worse, they found that when things did move, when the UN and Bangladesh signed agreements on repatriation with Myanmar, they were not called upon for their opinion. The decisions were made for them, as they always had been.

REORGANISING

Of course, there had been Rohingya civil society groups in the camps before and there had been political wings of the resistance groups able to engage with Bangladesh in 1978 and the 1990s. Though the government saw them as a useful connection to the community, it had always been easy to throw them all into prison on trumped-up charges when their demands seemed inconvenient or were simply rendered irrelevant by political interests and diplomatic wrangling. There was never any international outcry, no news coverage to prompt pressure. Their civil society was active but, without ways to engage others, it had little voice or leverage. This new iteration that presented itself had more options. Though their attempts to talk to the government and UN had hardly been any more fruitful, the protesters now have the option to use the internet. It allows them to coordinate their responses on Facebook or in WhatsApp groups, to set up meetings at short notice and to keep in constant conversation with key contacts they know are able and willing to amplify their concerns. It is also a direct line to the world. Generally, the Rohingya are most familiar with Facebook, which has connected broken families across the continent, but the youngest activists learn the importance of Twitter— the place where diplomats post their selfies from Kutupalong and journalists scour for information. Only a decade earlier, Zia and Nobi could only meet influential people in carefully curated situations, scrutinised by Nayapara's watchful and vengeful camp authorities. Now that can be bypassed for direct contact that allows them to be more frank. Those who are too loud can still be scolded in the CiC's office, but chucking them into a cell cannot be done without someone noticing.

So, this demonstration on the hills is the chance to take a hold of the narrative. Instead of relying on the local media's coverage and interpretation of events, they put out statements, tweet images and share videos that make world news. It is a victory of sorts, a statement that Rohingya voices exist and are more than meek respondents in interviews or surveys passed off by humanitarian agencies as community participation. Behind the scenes there is a mini army of young Rohingya making it all work, who have rough English skills they refine with camp visitors and whose minds constantly develop new digital strategies for their advocacy. Their skills frustrated by life in Bangladesh, they are energised by the opportunity to work towards something—leading the publicity charge but also organising their own generation for the protest. Their elders held meetings, but these young men combine social media broadcasting with old-fashioned campaigning on the streets, walking between camps, engaging other youth at tea shops and wherever they can find them. They establish their own networks, born mostly online but finding physical form in group meetings held in cramped, hot rooms that some of them had to make long journeys to reach. The logistical difficulties are outweighed by the purpose they feel. Most are boys but, with encouragement, a few young women join as well. Most work on education, others collate reports of problems in the camps and track cases of human trafficking. One group gathers every week to study various pieces of international law with the goal of preparing themselves with the legal knowledge they might need to argue the Rohingya case to the world. The most distinct group being formed is led by Chekufa, a young Rohingya woman from a middle-class family in Rakhine, who studied at Sittwe University until 2012. She established a group of twenty women, who then in their own camps established their own groups of twenty, thus forming a large umbrella group focused on raising women's education levels but also easily mobilised for activism. On the day of the 25 August memorial, they storm through the bazaar with a banner: "365 days of crying, now I am angry."

Mohibullah

More publicly, the image of Rohingya civil society has settled on one man: Mohibullah. He is a short, almost timid man on first meeting, always warm to his guests at his Kutupalong office. An ignorant eye could easily miss the office, hidden between shelters and behind the workshop of a Rohingya tailor, whose forever clacking sewing machine is all that is noticeable about that row of huts. The room is a relatively large and open space, decorated with banners announcing the slogans of his group, the Arakan Rohingya Society for Peace and Human Rights (ARSPH). "No NVC, No Bangali" is written in red; "Yes Rohingya" in green. Next to it is a list of fourteen demands, including citizenship and safety in Rakhine before they can agree to return, as well as requests for a UN security force, war crimes prosecutions against Tatmadaw generals and the closure of the heavily policed displacement camps in Sittwe. The only furnishings are a single desk at the front and a stack of plastic chairs that rarely accommodate everyone in the room. Instead, UNHCR-branded floor mats host cross-legged *majhis* and other community representatives who regularly walk or bus in from even the furthest camps to consider the proposals Mohibullah has been working on to unite the Rohingya. Even before they planned the anniversary memorial, this room was used by ARSPH to organise a campaign to count the victims of 25 August. The official death toll had not moved beyond the 6,700 estimated by MSF based on surveys in September, when the Rohingya themselves were still in chaos, but Mohibullah's team felt there needed to be something more substantial. They connected with the *majhis* and used the mini army of young volunteers to tread the camp's dirt paths, spreading as far and wide as possible to carry out a survey of the dead. They spent hours in shelters asking their inhabitants about what had happened in their villages, about their lost family members. They were able to get to a figure of 10,000 killed and linked those numbers to names, locations and family histories. The work set the foundations for ARSPH, propelling them to the forefront of Rohingya civil society and earning them the respect of other refugees. It gave Mohibullah enough standing that people would listen to him, even when ARSPH decided their activities needed to take on a stronger stance that might irritate their Bangladeshi hosts. Their early days had only been about social work in the camps and advocating for justice against Myanmar—for Bangladesh, they had only words of gratitude.

Mohibullah and ARSPH now realise their problems are not short-term and acquiescence is not going to help them return to Rakhine in a way that would not mean fleeing to Bangladesh again, whether in a few years or a decade. They cannot again meekly accept everything that is thrown at them. It had taken Bangladesh only a couple of months to agree a pact with Myanmar for repatriation and Rohingya activist circles were soon alerted to murmurs of an agreement with the UN, on which they had not been consulted. While Bangladesh's dealings were concerning, to have the UN also negotiating for the Rohingya made them feel completely abandoned. They were, of course, told there was no reason to worry, but a leaked version of a preliminary Memorandum of Understanding (MOU) eventually confirmed their fears—it was eerily similar to past agreements when nothing addressed their demands for citizenship. There was a vague reference to some sort of identification that sounded all too similar to the NVC cards. Clearly, the parties had not noted the observations of the shelved 2010 report on UNHCR's role in the 1978 and 1990s repatriations, which said physically returning the Rohingya did not solve their crisis as long as they remained stateless—without the "right to have rights".

They could return the Rohingya to relative quiet in northern Rakhine State, but it did not mean they had peace.

The MOU was also proof that the UN were not noting the demands in offices like Mohibullah's, where "No NVC" banners are proudly displayed. Even after the 25 August demonstrations and their show of Rohingya unity, the humanitarians have still treated Rohingya civil society as fringe and unrepresentative. Though they were unable to organise the widespread elections they had promised, they insisted those they spoke to should be democratically elected. That meant they spoke to no one. They also did not consult the Rohingya when UNHCR and Bangladesh put together a new identity system based on what came to be known as "smart cards". The 2017 mass arrivals had prompted a hasty process to count all the new refugees—even the "hunger refugees" who had spent a decade invisible—but the process also had holes and there were concerns about how robust the registration was. The new biometric process would mean registering everyone again, but this time taking their fingerprints, eye scans and details of their villages back in Myanmar. It felt intrusive and Rohingya activists were suspicious about whether it could link to repatriations and the NVC system. Worse was the chance that this information could fall into Myanmar's hands and be used to lash out against critics and any relatives still in Myanmar.

These fears have prompted Mohibullah to call the camp leaders back to his office. They arrive, as usual, by foot or bus or in packed electric rickshaws and sit, as usual, cross-legged on the floor. Mohibullah stands at the front chewing betel nut while some of the curious local elders sit outside, peering in through the woven bamboo walls. He speaks for a long time, around an hour, and everyone listens attentively to his soft but assured voice. A few raise questions, but his concerns about the dangers of the data falling into Myanmar's hands are compelling. He issues a rallying call and they all agree—they will go on strike. They have already been refusing to sign up for the cards unless consulted and their refusal has been frustrating the authorities. A few very isolated camps south of Nayapara have taken the cards because of rumours they would be allowed to move freely beyond the camps, and threats made by some workers that they would be denied food. But, by and large, no one is signing up.

Months after UNHCR announced the programme, less than 2 per cent of the refugees had signed up, but UNHCR still wanted to push on.

10

REPATRIATION AND REPRESSION

November 2018

An unnamed woman steps out of the darkness, her face hidden behind a yellow scarf, screaming directly at the mobile phone. The rude light on its rear side is the only illumination in the camp's total darkness, allowing her to be seen as she sends her desperate warning. It arrives on the phones of refugees in other camps as a grainy video. They cannot read the fear from her concealed face but it is there in her voice, dripping from her words about the men she says are waiting in the darkness behind her, invisible to the camera. "They have surrounded our camp from all corners ... RAB [Rapid Action Battalion] and others have surrounded us, they don't allow us to eat. They want to take the people away tonight. That's why we are very scared and informing you all." The last words overwhelm her and she slams shut her eyes, as if to fight back tears, then raises her hand to hide them and signal the end of the message.

The video was shot in Unchiparang, one of the camps singled out to provide 485 families for the first round of repatriation, agreed between Myanmar and Bangladesh a few weeks earlier. A cordon had been set up around their encampment, building the sense of doom that grew with the approach of the repatriation deadline. Though it was known that Bangladesh had signed repatriation agreements and gestured about its readiness to push the process through, the prospect had never seemed so real. Every week 150 refugees were supposed to cross. Myanmar said it would process them at its Nga Khu Ya reception camp and then move them all on to Hla Poe Kaung, a massive new transit camp built on the site of two destroyed Rohingya villages. Fenced in by barbed wire like the internment camps near Sittwe, it is a complex of tin-roofed bungalows that could house 25,000 people. It was supposed to be temporary, but Myanmar had given no indication of where the returnees would go from here. Their homes had not been rebuilt. Grass was growing over the ruins of some. Military barracks now stood on others.

No one had made it clear to the refugees that any of this was voluntary. Reason suggested it would be, that not enough time had passed for Bangladesh to claim it was safe enough that they could be forced back, but the confusion suited authorities who probably hoped at least a few hundred refugees might follow along and leave, setting the process in motion. The UN, maybe caught a little off guard themselves, stood by and observed, offering nothing to help clear the air. Their own agreements with Myanmar meant the refugees had no reason to believe the UN was not involved in all of this anyway—especially for those who remembered the 1990s. A forced repatriation would grab headlines and surely drown Bangladesh in condemnation, but it was too dangerous for the refugees to doubt the threat. *Majhis* had been given names and informed the listed families, who did not hesitate in abandoning their shelters. They took little with them, walking over to stay with relatives somewhere else in the camp where it would be too hard to track them down, or even turning to the same forests most had sheltered in when they first arrived in Bangladesh before the camps took shape. It was cold and strange in the woods, but hiding in them felt all too reminiscent of the days spent hiding from the Myanmar military. Some left children behind in the care of neighbours to spare them the unknown dangers of the wilderness, hoping the government would not dare seize unaccompanied children. By the time buses rolled up outside the camps on 15 November, very few of the 485 families were left in their shelters.

By then, most Rohingya throughout the camps had heard about Dil Mohammed, though they may not have known his name. A wiry, nervous man, he had become more concerned with each day that brought the deadline closer—especially when old women started to arrive in his block with stories of police intimidating them. His concern peaked the day before the repatriation, when he was told by his local *majhi* that he was on the list and realised the same officers might soon be turning up at his shelter. He was determined not to go but decided to discuss it with his wife Hamida, who surprised him. She said she would like to return home. She was not altogether serious, but even the suggestion was enough to rile her husband. Her argument, that dying at home could be no worse than dying in exile, hit Dil Mohammed as serious. In the back room of their shelter, more spacious than others because he had bought it from a longer-settled refugee, their strained debate was heard by all the neighbours through the plastic boundaries of their homes, until they reached deadlock and Hamida abandoned the conversation. She went to pray, laying out her prayer mat completely unaware that her husband was stewing in his thoughts—internally wracked by the pain of the decision, by the concept of returning. She was still in prayer, prostrating, when he was suddenly overwhelmed and in panic gulped down the remains of a bottle of insecticide left over from the insect-ridden monsoon months. He was soon writhing around on the floor, in such pain that he could not remember what followed. Hamida panicked, unaware of what had brought on his sudden illness or how to treat it. She screamed for the neighbours and traditional healers, who tried to flush his body with a drink made from a ground leaf they use to absorb toxins. It failed, so they called on the local youth to stretcher him through the darkness to a camp clinic.

The photo that circulated on the day of the repatriation showed Dil Mohammed laid out on a hospital bed, eyes closed. It was attached to rumours of his death that spread like wildfire, setting the glum tone for a morning already darkened by the previous night's video of the veiled woman warning of the police siege. Dil Mohammed's desperation was shocking, but not altogether surprising, because he had only attempted what many had warned of whenever the idea of returning to Myanmar was raised: they would rather die. During the whole period, there had been nowhere for them to turn for clear information. They heard only the rumours of intimidation, families fleeing and names on lists handed to *majhis*. Though civil society had shown in August its ability to organise, it was not enough to be granted a seat at the table. The activists could rally the Rohingya around resisting repatriation, but they could not promise it would not happen by force; they knew nothing more than anyone else. UNHCR were silent. They had been caught off-guard by the process, barely consulted by the government, but had themselves also barely said anything to the Rohingya—apparently paralysed and hoping Bangladesh's brinkmanship would not teeter into forced deportations. The UN dealt with the issue a long way from the camps, in the conference rooms in Cox's Bazar luxury hotels, without a single Rohingya present. They chose silence over communication, but created a hotline that individual refugees could phone for advice. In reality, the line appeared to be manned by a single person, who was barely trained and asked personal questions more likely to spook enquiring refugees than

comfort them. It may have been decades since the last repatriations from Bangladesh, but UNHCR, whose own workers were
aware they had failed, were not ready to support the refugees.

By midday on the day of the repatriation, the drivers of the
three buses and four trucks idling at the entrance to Unchiparang
had already spent hours waiting under the sun. They were supposed to be carting twenty-seven families away, but the UN could
find only a few on the list who made it clear they did not want to
return. These vehicles had arrived after dawn and immediately
became a spectacle watched by the media, monitored by activists
and eyed warily by refugees picking up aid from the nearby supply
point. Small crowds gathered at a distance, watching for activity
beyond the drivers' impatient pacing and bored drags on cigarettes. They waited for the moment families would be forced
aboard. Elsewhere, a few organised by civil society groups pro-
tested and filmed their message to be shared online. The tense
stand-off continued late into the evening, when the Refugee
Relief and Repatriation Commissioner (RRRC) Abul Kalam
finally admitted defeat: the repatriation was being called off.

The relief was immediate, but his announcement was laced
with warning. Though Bangladesh would not be forcing anyone
to leave, Abul Kalam said that it would continue to motivate the
refugees to return of their own accord. Though the commissioner himself was well liked, the motivation he had in mind had
little to do with making Myanmar more liveable, which was
beyond Bangladesh's control, and would take a long time to
implement. The failed repatriation was a small victory of resistance for the refugees, but did nothing to improve their relations
with their hosts. Bangladesh was tiring of the refugees and there
was growing pressure to move them on again. Though locals had
been the first to save the refugees arriving on their borders a year
earlier, they had tired of the disruption to their lives. Costs had
gone up and there was more pressure on already scarce water

supplies and other resources. Fuel had not been among the supplies provided by the NGOs, so forests had been cut down for firewood. Once a relatively quiet place, Teknaf Road had been torn up by heavy vehicles and a long file of minibuses that extended travel times by hours. These half-empty transports and their foreign passengers became targets for a group of agitators who formed a consortium demanding more jobs. They staged strikes and harangued foreign workers—who they believed offered very little while being paid to stay in luxury hotels—at Court Bazar, where their vehicles joined Teknaf Road from the more exclusive, traffic-free Marine Drive. Local newspapers championed their cause, attaching it to a larger discussion on the aid community's neglect of Bangladeshi NGOs. But they also returned to their old tropes about the Rohingya, the ones the community had long bought into but had set aside during 2017's disaster. One local journalist shared a video he claimed showed Rohingya making weapons in the camps, in a project funded by an NGO. In reality, it was a tool shop, crafting the machetes the Rohingya used for repairing their homes and gathering fuel. He had posted on Facebook, ensuring that not just his usual readership of Cox's Bazar newspapers but the whole country was sharing rumours about the Rohingya arming themselves.

The nation had been busy until now flaunting its own generosity towards the Rohingya, and so it was easy for a few videos and carefully placed news reports to flip that narrative into Rohingya ingratitude. This disinformation worked domestically and also bought it space internationally as it began preparing policies that would achieve the so-called "motivation" for the Rohingya to repatriate. Bangladesh was helped by its neighbour India also happily peddling stories of Rohingya conspiracy so that it could also deport them. Sheikh Hasina's government revived the 2015 idea of rehousing refugees on the floating island, Bhasan Char, as an alternative to repatriation. It had always been rubbished internationally as a dangerous and impractical concept, but Bangladesh wanted to prove it could work. It hired a British company to engineer flood protections and went ahead with building housing compounds that, from appearance alone, were clearly superior to the shacks the Rohingya had been housed in until now. Twenty years ago, there had been literally nothing in this part of the Bay of Bengal; now a town had emerged on this collection of silt deposits. A polished promotional film was shown in the camps, the authorities hoping the impressive new homes would be enough to swing tearoom debates about the move, which had always been vehemently opposed. But the authorities also left the issue of consent ambiguous. They were trying to entice volunteers but there was no real effort to clarify whether it would still go ahead if none were found. Perhaps they thought the fear of wasting away in a remote prison would be a motivator for returning to Myanmar—a second pressure point. Ministers began alternating between announcements about preparing to move people to Bhasan Char and of plans for repatriations, the two working in tandem to ensure there was forever a threat looming over the Rohingya. The international community issued statements objecting, but as Bangladesh grew more forthright some of that opposition softened into public reservation and became conditional. The UN stopped saying they rejected the idea outright and instead demanded a chance to at least inspect the island before action was taken.

Nobi

"Remember, God is never far", Nobi leans in and whispers. A few days earlier his face was tired, but now it has slightly lightened after the morning's news that the shadow hanging over Nayapara has lifted. It is a warm evening sat out in the open in

Cox's Bazar and, thanks to a training programme that allowed him to be in town, Nobi can finally relax a little. Now that it is in the news anyway, he can finally speak the name of Nurul Alam, the Rohingya gun peddler shot dead that morning. His death was announced by Bangladeshi forces, who described him as a wanted militant they had tracked down to the hills behind Nayapara, where he had triggered a shootout and been killed. Bangladeshis were indifferent; they had heard before this kind of story with the typical descriptions of "gunfights" and "crossfire", but sympathy was unlikely now the idea of violent, armed Rohingya militants and drug traffickers had been normalised. There was also little concern from the Rohingya themselves, who had seen other such crossfires as injustice. Nurul Alam had been a terror to his neighbours. Local newspaper reports called him an ARSA member and though it was true that he had been in Rakhine with them, even pictured in the background of one of the initial videos announcing their presence, Nurul Alam was no idealist to the Rohingya who knew him. Like Nobi, he had grown up in Nayapara but on a different path, drawn into the camp underbelly that was cultivated by Teknaf's crime networks. He and friends picked up jobs for local criminals, as runners or enforcers, but over time grew into their own little gang able to pull off their own heists. They picked up weapons and found ways to steal more from Bangladeshi authorities. It was thought that he had been behind an ambush on a Bangladeshi post that secured some of the few firearms used by ARSA in October 2016. Nobi was surprised when he saw Nurul Alam appear as an ARSA member, presenting himself as a man of noble goals, but any idea that he had changed was dispelled when he returned to Bangladesh as ARSA went into hiding. He was often found drunk, bullying young refugees who dared to play football too close to territory he had unilaterally declared his own. His return was followed by an arrest for the attack on the Bangladeshi security forces—though he was released within a year, despite the severity of the accusation, and went into hiding near Nayapara.

Nurul Alam's death had struck Nobi because only a few days earlier he had been completely exasperated by the man. He could not yet speak openly, but he had decided, for the first time, to take advantage of the safety Cox's Bazar offered from prying ears to open up about what was happening in the camps. "In every camp there are these people who say they are ARSA, and they're dangerous", said Nobi. "I've seen it myself, them attacking people as I walked past. This has become habitual for them. What we know as ARSA, they are criminals. Look at the Arakan Army, you see them building a headquarters and a way to fight. These people couldn't even stay two days in the fight— it's just a tale for the people. They're busy working as criminals, sending people to carry Yaba tablets to different parts of the country or snatching our own people to demand money from them. They don't have the capacity to do anything against Myanmar, they're only able to kill their own people, to harass their own people. If I spoke about this there, back in that camp, this same night I would be no more."

Though far from Nayapara, Nobi still pauses between words, struggling with the internal safeguards that have taught him to hold his tongue inside the camp and scanning the crowd to register who else is nearby. He has decided to open up, but the words are not easy to draw out. He has not spoken about ARSA to an outsider for a while, not since journalists rushed in hoping for a scoop on a shadowy militant organisation sitting in the camps. They apparently expected ARSA to be waiting in Bangladesh, drawing on the anger of victims to recruit members and immediately launch an insurgency against the Myanmar army. Most of the reporting rested on assumptions made during the past two decades of post-9/11 reporting on Muslims and violence, which assumed that ARSA were popular, that they were known among the Rohingya and that there was a "both-sides" story to be told about radicalisation and an Islamist threat to Rakhine. Many of the humanitarians came with similar assumptions, linking any sign of conservatism to ARSA. But unlike the Afghan and Syrian comparisons they seemed to be drawing from, there was no sustained outside funding for ARSA, no protection under the wing of a foreign intelligence agency. If there had been, ARSA may have used more than a mob and crude weapons in its rare assaults on the Myanmar army. The camps of eastern Bangladesh were also not the camps of eastern Congo, where Rwandan *génocidaires* had infamously disguised themselves among refugees. The people now living in Bangladesh were still scared and completely exhausted, with no energy to join a fight against Myanmar even if they had been approached for recruitment. So, it was hard for journalists to find their interviewees.

The last time Nobi had spoken openly about ARSA, he had been presented as a member of the group in an American broad-caster's report. His face was blurred but his voice was unmasked, easily identified by friends abroad who were immediately worried about the danger he could face from intelligence authorities. Only a year earlier he had been detained just for helping a small foreign charity. Though the reporter described him as an ARSA member, he had never actually told her that he was. He was asked whether, generally, he thought the Rohingya had a right to defend themselves. He answered in English that some "other Rohingya" saw ARSA as the only group willing to die for their rights, while they had been forsaken by the international community. Like most others, his opinion on ARSA had vacillated over time. There had to be some hope somewhere, and why should the Rohingya not have means to defend themselves? Their neighbours in Rakhine State had the far more sophisti-cated Arakan Army, which inflicted heavy and regular losses on the Burmese army, while full-blown rebellions against the state raged on Myanmar's other frontiers, supported from abroad without fear of being slapped with the war-on-terror narrative that cropped up whenever Muslims were involved. But it was hard to ignore what ARSA's failures had cost the Rohingya while delivering no progress. Whatever ARSA was supposed to represent no longer mattered. Nobi was not alone in hearing the things that were happening in their name. There were more and more whispers about them by people eager to talk— volunteering their grievances when they were safe, passing them on to their relatives further abroad—though even in the small shops in Kuala Lumpur their original name, Al-Yaqeen, was mentioned only in whispers. In Myanmar, the group had been almost unheard of for more than a year. There were occasional appearances on social media, tweets or recorded messages in reaction to repatriation measures, critical of Myanmar and the humanitarian agencies but cautious about addressing Bangladesh's role. Few knew exactly what they were or how they were run—the rest could see only a group, or perhaps other groups using their name to borrow credibility or besmirch their reputation, harassing the people they said they fought for. The group's core members were hidden somewhere in the frontier hills, training and biding their time, while the more politically inclined sat in third countries.

* * *

Any sense of relief encouraged by Nurul Alam's removal, however does not last the night. Instead of going into hiding, his men wait until darkness falls to grab their weapons and storm down from the forest with their message. With no fear of consequence, they barge into shelters, harass shopkeepers and beat fear into anyone they cross. Nobi's phone is pinging with alerts on their movements, delivered in almost real time by the trail of witnesses and victims surviving this rampage and wanting to warn others of what is coming. Nobi shifts uncomfortably in his seat, struggling to look away from his phone but fearing what he might read next. Nurul Alam's friends do not have the means to respond to the Bangladeshi security forces, which would have been a declaration of war, so seek their revenge from those who can offer no response or resistance. If delinquent youth are their recruitment pool, then it is the aspirational young, those who speak other languages and work with aid workers, who the bandits see as potential informants. A few others on the same training course are all receiving the same messages as Nobi, his and their faces growing graver the more they read. An hour passes with Nobi sat fidgeting, nervously glancing at his phone every few minutes in case there is a new notification. There is talk of shootings, of several people injured. One has been taken to hospital. His name is Hasan, the man who runs the computer shop. He is well known to the community, a leader in his block and well educated. Then comes word of Mohamed Hamid, a 41-year-old first aid provider. He is confirmed dead.

What Nobi had been trying to say before that night was that they were everywhere. They had taken time to reveal themselves, but when they did it was an abrasive change for the other Rohingya: a challenge to a civil society that had focused on education, advocacy and political unity, even if these had always been hard to achieve. Now gangs dressed their activity in fancy words and were trying to force that unity. What most saw were mere gaggles of young delinquents, with little power otherwise, who had taken it upon themselves to implement a petty shadow government, mostly in the extended Kutupalong camp system. They were not necessarily creations of ARSA, but swore allegiance to the group. They arbitrarily attempted to enforce conservative moral codes on women who worked, claiming they were corrupted by outside influences, and harassed young activists or community leaders they saw as opponents. They were little more than a nuisance themselves, but drew confidence from their more experienced commanders, who sat in the background and tried to build up authority. Though ARSA projected a clean image, those who represented them, like Nurul Alam and Yaba-linked Master Munna, had shady backgrounds that provided useful revenue streams. They presented themselves as respectable men, often spending money in the community or on mosques while young henchmen bullied the rest into submission, insisting *majhis* report to these leaders and searching the phones of whoever they suspected might be sharing critical views. They soon had much of Kutupalong under their thumb, operating at night without interference from security forces who rarely ventured beyond the camp's entrances. In reality, there were actually several groups competing for influence and using abductions as their main means of intimidation. They kidnapped each other and they kidnapped any they felt needed to fall in line. When their warnings to female aid workers to stop working did not get through, they seized them, taking them to remote locations outside the camp where they were forced to watch their relatives bound and beaten. Some were taken and returned the same night; others went missing for longer stretches or never returned.

The highest-profile victim was an imam seized from his home while he was praying at night. Back in July 2018, it was one of the earliest announcements of ARSA's reach: a response to a religious ruling he had helped draft in opposition to their tactics. This argued the Rohingya were too weak to mount operations against the Burmese military and so any action right now would only lead to the "Muslims demolishing themselves fighting with knives, sticks and stones". Another forty Rohingya religious leaders signed the document, which was the most vocal anyone had been in opposition to ARSA since the 2017 expulsion though it did not directly criticise them. Not only did the ruling voice a widespread Rohingya complaint, it was made by a force strong enough to undermine them. ARSA never commented on the imam's disappearance, but as they grew stronger some of their members were rumoured to have bragged about killing him—an example of the reach they had and the lengths they were willing to go to. His body was never found but those of other critical religious leaders were later discovered by police, beaten and bloated after days or weeks undetected in the long grass.

Kidnappings offered more than a chance to intimidate opponents, they could be used for financial benefit as well. Aside from kidnappings by ARSA's members, its smaller rivals used their own relative anonymity among the community to claim actions in ARSA's name, taking the financial reward without the reputational damage. The small power gained by joining these gang-like structures may have been the main appeal to the recruited youth, but they could also wield it for financial benefit. ARSA, however, denied any link to any of this. They railed against drug smuggling and human trafficking in statements. When Fortify Rights pinned abductions of female aid workers on them, they issued a statement denying it all, blaming rival groups intent on besmirching their name, while insisting they were committed to human rights laws. They warned, however, that their followers should avoid crime.

* * *

The sight of Bangladeshi soldiers deep inside Kutupalong, rifles slung from their bodies, was new. They had always been present at the entrances by a sort of consensus, involved wherever aid was supplied and infrastructure work carried out. They had been appreciated for the helping hands they extended to refugees stumbling through August's and September's swampy fields. Nurul Alam's killing meant they took on a new appearance as a patrolling force, one present not to support the refugees but with a mission to search for threats lurking in the camps. Initially, it was probably little more than a symbolic move: a signal to ARSA and any other group that Bangladesh would not tolerate any headaches—especially ones that might disturb the local community, whose religious leaders shared ties with the Rohingya's and who were also facing intimidation. That same week there had also been a ruckus over a mob physically ripping apart a vehicle carrying three German journalists. It was caused by a misunderstanding: a group of mistrustful refugees feared that the foreigners, who had a Rohingya woman and her children in their car, were human traffickers. They were given no explanation from the Bangladeshi translator—a journalist from Dhaka who shouted at them in Bengali instead of Rohingya. The journalists were left bruised and the humanitarian community panicked. Worried workers shared a Google Translate version of a local media report on the incident. Some speculated, as they tended to, that it might be the result of some kind of radicalisation among the refugees. Bangladesh was angry and sent patrols into the camps to make arrests, but found the pathways near Lambashia, where the incident had occurred, were deserted. The market was not running that day and the shopkeepers had pulled down and padlocked the thin metal sheets that protected their bamboo structures. All but a young pharmacist, treating a patient's stomach problems with a saline drip strung from his shop's low roof, had locked themselves at home, fearing that anyone caught out would be detained to make up the numbers. Young activists quickly issued a statement begging forgiveness for the misunderstanding. Unlike the aid workers and Bangladeshi reporters, they had actually been there and seen the confusion but still deferred to the prevailing narrative, worried about how it would harm perspectives about the refugees.

The real changes to come had nothing to do with that incident, nor really with the abductions and accusations against

ARSA. They would have little to do with Kutupalong either, where the government had barely put any thought into security but was planning to build a wire fence around the camps to ensure that movement was controlled even more. Although not the first crossfire, Nurul Alam's death had put a spotlight on insecurity in the camps. The security forces reacted and focused on the southern camps around Nayapara. The residents grew used to soldiers from the nearby barracks rolling past in pick-up trucks, armed and helmeted, as though on a mission. They also heard more about crossfires in the nearby forests. In those same places, or on the concrete by schools or police checkpoints, they began to find the bodies of young men who had gone missing. They were always accompanied by a story in the press.

11

CRACKDOWN

August 2019

At first sight, it was a peaceful image. Untouched greenery filled the eye and mountains loomed in the background, beyond the river that wrapped around empty fields. This young, wild vegetation was neither forest nor farmland—it had grown atop Tula Toli.

The signs were there on closer inspection. The bamboo supporting pillars of burnt-out houses still jutted out from the untamed bush as the last evidence that the village had existed. "This is my grandmother's home", a boy filming says to the camera. "Look at the state of it after the authorities torched our homes." Birds chirp and insects buzz in the background, sounds only so audible when a village is asleep. The boys wander through the shrubbery, soaking in the sight of their abandoned homes and looking, until night falls, for the mass graves under the new grass. The boys decided to make the trip, to become the first to see Tula Toli when all others were turned away on approach, when they saw cattle arriving in Bangladesh branded with the marks of Tula Toli farmers, sold on by whoever had appropriated the Rohingya property. "We didn't manage to come earlier because the military dogs were around", they said. "See what they have done. Get angry."

* * *

The ghostly peace in abandoned Tula Toli was not shared by the Rohingya villages that remained inhabited. Two years on, there were still fires burning. Houses and mosques were being flattened by shelling, young children hit with shrapnel. They were not officially the targets, but fighting still raged around them despite ARSA having practically disappeared from the scene. Rakhine's few remaining Rohingya were caught up in a war fought by the Tatmadaw and the Arakan Army, which with thousands of trained fighters, modern weapons and base camps in the hills possessed tools Rohingya rebels had only dreamed of. While the Tatmadaw had been busy ridding Rakhine of the Rohingya, the Arakan Army had spent the decade since their founding preparing a far more serious threat to Myanmar's control, stashing weapons in underground forest bunkers in Bangladesh's Chittagong Hill Tracts and training and fighting alongside the Kachin Independence Army on another of Myanmar's frontiers. They had been poking the Burmese military machine since 2015, but on 4 January 2019 killed thirteen soldiers in an attack that prompted the Tatmadaw to again announce clearance operations—this time claiming the orders had come directly from Aung San Suu Kyi herself. She declared them a terrorist group and demanded the army "defeat them effectively, quickly and clearly", according to a military spokesman. The military did what it was used to and headed for Rakhine villages, punishing the inhabitants they claimed were sheltering the Arakan Army guerrillas. It was the same reasoning they had used to tear through Rohingya villages only two years earlier. Schools and clinics were hit, and villagers spent curfewed nights huddled together in hiding.[1] The government tried to strangle the flow of information with an internet blackout over rural Rakhine, but journalists transferred videos and their reports onto physical discs and smuggled them by bus to the nearest safe internet connection in Sittwe, although this could be days away. The Arakan Army also found ways of getting material out to their supporters abroad, who pushed out images reminiscent of 2017—of families fleeing their homes with babies strapped to their backs, crafting rafts from bamboo to escape across rivers. At first, they asked why there was no outrage for the Rakhine as there had been for the Rohingya, but were surprised by sympathy shown by Rohingya activists online who argued this was the moment for unity against Tatmadaw brutality that could touch all in Rakhine State, not just its Muslim minority. There had been calls for pan-Rakhine unity in the past and, for a time, some discussed whether shared oppression might finally make that a reality. For now, there seemed to be unity in death. The Rohingya were not involved in the fight, but they were still being killed. Many struggled to believe they were only being caught in the crossfire. The horrors often crashed down on them at night—as they did on 3 April, when a helicopter buzzed over Hpon Nyo Leik in Buthidaung and opened fire on villagers in their fields. Seven Rohingya civilians were killed. Around 4,000 left this village alone over a few days, camping on the road as they headed westward, to Bangladesh.[2, 3]

Despite documenting the massacre, the UN reported to Bangladesh that same month that conditions in Rakhine had improved. This judgement drew incredulous responses from refugee activists who had intently followed the news coming from their old homes, from relatives still trapped. The Tatmadaw themselves had recognised the area was not safe for repatriation, though only so it could blame the Arakan Army for destabilising the region. It conveniently allowed Myanmar a way to escape its responsibilities while again playing Rakhine's two major communities off against each other. The second anniversary of the 25 August massacres was approaching and, aside from the violence, no progress had been made in building Rohingya villages back up and there was no sign that the country would grant the refugees their core demand of being recognised as citizens.

There had been some preliminary contact between Myanmar and the Rohingya, but no progress on citizenship. China stepped in on Myanmar's behalf and supposedly offered to pay the Rohingya up to $6,000 each if they accepted a return without making demands. Mohibullah made their offer public and insisted the Rohingya would return for safety but not for money. Citizenship was crucial. Bangladesh officially supported the linkage of repatriation to citizenship, but had little leverage to force any change without international support on the issue. The international community seemed content with the Rohingya remaining in place, neither putting any pressure on Myanmar to improve conditions nor offering to host refugees themselves. It also continued to oppose a move to Bhasan Char, which seemed to most Bangladeshis a perfect solution with housing that seemed better than their own. It could have pressured Myanmar through the business channels that had been opened as a reward for the elections that brought Aung San Suu Kyi into power, but that would have meant the EU and United States inconveniencing themselves. ASEAN had shifted its policy of non-interference to one of active support for Myanmar, producing a report from Rakhine State that could not bear to name the Rohingya other than as Muslims. They claimed Myanmar had tried to "facilitate a smooth repatriation process". There was not a single sign of meaningful change, and this was wearing at the patience of both the hosts and refugees. Bangladesh was in no mood to receive more refugees—neither from the new conflict in Rakhine State nor from India, whence Rohingya were still fleeing, having decided their welcome had ended under Modi's rule. Bangladesh began to reject them at the border, leaving them stuck in no man's land. It wanted to show it would not become a place for every Rohingya to be sent to when other host countries decided they were unwanted. Hindu nationalist Indian social media trolls used the images of stranded refugees to claim the opposite was happening—that Bangladesh was unleashing a torrent of Muslims to overwhelm Hindu lands—to feed anti-Rohingya sentiment even further.

Mohibullah

Mohibullah discovered the world's indifference in person. Dressed in a greyish suit and striped tie, he stood in the Oval Office and listened to an Uyghur woman tell Donald Trump how China had rounded up more than a million of her people, including her own father, in massive detention camps in western China. In the room were representatives from sixteen countries, all from persecuted religious minorities and gathered to meet the American president. They were fanned out behind and to the sides of Trump's desk, an arrangement suited for the cameras but which meant Trump often had his back turned to them during the brief moment each had to capture his attention. Mohibullah listened patiently to the others speak with his hands folded into each other, resting on his stomach, and raised his hand politely when the Uyghur woman finished and it was his turn. He fiddled nervously with the hem of his jacket as he introduced himself as a Rohingya refugee, emphasised how much they would like to return home and asked Trump what the plan to help them is. "And where is that exactly?" Trump responded, causing Mohibullah's grin to instantly collapse. Standing by Trump's side, his envoy for religious freedoms, Ambassador Sam Brownback, informed the president that it was "next to Burma". Trump nodded, as if in recognition, said "thanks" and moved on to a Cuban man. Mohibullah forced another smile. One of Mohibullah's assistants who had travelled with him came away from his trip to America with only a single lasting takeaway: how strikingly stupid Trump was. It was disappointing that the president had not only shown no interest but could not even recognise the Rohingya name, despite them being burned out of their homes during his term as president.

After two years of campaigning for a chance to speak, there were some in the humanitarian agencies who had tried to facilitate it, to get Rohingya civil society leaders into places where they might be heard. It had taken an enormous amount of persuading to get Bangladesh to allow the travel and grant documents, yet all they found was more disappointment at the end of those air journeys. Mohibullah and women from Shanti Mohilla, which had focused on women's justice, had also been let down months earlier, when in March they were taken to Geneva to speak to the human rights council. Mohibullah was cut off two minutes into his speech, just as he was going to bring up the UN's lack of consultation with the Rohingya over repatriation. The UN's custom on allowing two minutes for submissions was apparently too rigid to allow survivors, of violence the UN's own reports described as genocidal, to speak at any length. Shanti Mohilla's Hamida was not even given the chance to speak for herself. A translated version of her statement was read out for her. This was the world in which the Rohingya had believed decisions were made, where their testimonies collected by diplomats and researchers were filed. Mohibullah had visited this world now and found no answers. No one was even talking about them.

* * *

On 16 August 2019, the Bangladeshi government announced that it would again be launching the repatriation process.

Myanmar said it had approved 3,450 for arrival at the reception centre on the border. The UN had this time been informed before Bangladesh's announcement and prepared more of a plan, calling a meeting on how to devise their communications plan, which would kick in only three days before the deadline day on 22 August. Through these communications, they told the Rohingya that Myanmar's approval of individuals for repatriation was "a welcome first step as it acknowledges that your right to return is recognized". It also told them a repatriation would be voluntary and that they could speak to UNHCR officials and state whether they wanted to return and, if they did not, explain why. In private conversation, UNHCR officials admitted their lack of communications had meant some refugees thought they had no choice but to leave because of misinformation from *majhis*, who filled the gap. Rohingya were this time invited to meetings about how to consult the affected camps, whose names were added to the lists without being asked first, but the whole thing had been a surprise for them. A few civil society members were invited to give feedback to UNHCR, but far too late. They were once again the last to know about the coming repatriation and were surprised by it—especially as their leaders had only recently met Burmese representatives to negotiate terms for their return, with a follow-up meeting planned. Civil society had been quiet last time, without either the confidence or the reach to challenge the authorities, but decided it was necessary to show defiance now. The day before the repatriation, ARSPH and youth groups called a press conference in Nayapara, releasing the names of the refugees from nearby camps who were to be sent back. "We are very concerned about how this secret list was created and why we are included on it", they said, partnering their letter with their own lists of refugees who did not want to return, a thumbprint and signature confirming their stance. "We want to make it very clear to UNHCR, ASEAN, the Government of

Myanmar, and the Government of Bangladesh that there will be no repatriation without talking to us first."

The local media's obsession with the Rohingya was reaching fever pitch with the prospect of a Rohingya return, turning the event into something far bigger than it had been the year before. The day before, they carried numbers from the Bangladeshi police claiming there had been around 300 cases filed against Rohingya since 2017, including thirty murder cases. It was the perfect report to illustrate what trouble they were supposedly causing, though, in fact, the number was minuscule considering 700,000 Rohingya had arrived in that time. When the buses pulled up outside Nayapara, there was also a flock of journalists with them. Others went to the "friendship road"—a long stretch of immaculate tarmac just south of Kutupalong bazaar that was supposed to be the land path into Myanmar but was never used. These journalists brought their cameras and, more importantly, their phones for livestreaming, but they spent the day kicking dust once again. By the afternoon, the government admitted there were still no volunteers for return but ratcheted up the rhetoric. Where the RRRC had spoken before about motivating the Rohingya, Foreign Minister Abdul Momen appeared before reporters at 2.30 pm, blamed NGOs for convincing the Rohingya to stay and promised to root them out. He maintained that repatriations would be voluntary, but said the "comfort" the Rohingya were apparently living in would have to be reduced. It was an echo of the "fat, well-fed" refugees line from 1978, this time spoken in public rather than to a closed room of humanitarian workers.

Only three days later, the Rohingya were demonstrating out in their usual spots on the barren hills facing the border. The young dressed in their school uniforms again to mark the second anniversary of the 25 August massacres, and loudspeakers blared poems and speeches delivered to the crowd. There should have been no surprise about the protest. It went ahead with the permission of Bangladeshi authorities and followed the previous year's pattern. There was no criticism of Bangladesh, no expression of the fresh anger at another repatriation attempt. It would, however, change everything. It was the perfect example the government needed of the Rohingya being too comfortable, of resisting Bangladeshi wishes for their return and then staging a public protest. This was Rohingya ingratitude, the media blared. The official reaction was swift.

Nobi

After his morning lessons had finished and Nobi wandered down to the main road, he spotted on Nayapara's edges a few men, supervised by soldiers, busy at work. He had heard rumours of this. They had a pile of heavy fence posts and were hammering them into the ground, each post a similar distance from the other. The space in between them was empty but he quickly realised it was to be filled by tangled stretches of barbed wire. Nobi had known all his life that leaving the camps was forbidden, but this was the first time he had seen Bangladesh literally fence the Rohingya in. The plan was to confine the entirety of the camps but work was starting in Nayapara, where tensions with the host community were at their worst after a spate of crossfires. Not far north in Unchiparang, both locals and Rohingya were stopped by soldiers at the shared checkpoint for the Bangladeshi village and the refugee camp, forced to show their identity documents and open their belongings. Soldiers rifled through bags of personal items and, at their leisure and to their amusement, questioned enterprising businessmen about whether any of the hair products they were bringing in to sell were any good. Queues formed quickly.

This was the new regime, the idea of "less comfortable" realised. Within days, the usually bustling makeshift markets the

Rohingya had built up in the new camps were transformed into ghost towns. Where there had been vegetable hawkers, small egg hatcheries, tailors and blacksmiths, there were now only lines of metal shutters padlocked to the floor. Children spent the daytime loitering outside them and the elderly sat on their haunches watching not much pass by, while the owners sat in their homes waiting for night. Only then could they work without incurring the wrath of a new batch of CiCs, who had banned Rohingya business as Bangladesh decided it would no longer tolerate the exchange of cash between the refugees. It made them too comfortable, fuelled trafficking and was used to fraudulently buy paperwork that let refugees pass as Bangladeshi. This reasoning was set out officially in an order from the government's NGO bureau to end any cash incentives to Rohingya volunteers—they would have to be released or paid in rations. These new CiCs were part of a crackdown that was being linked to the 25 August memorial but was more about the failed repatriation. Their predecessors were blamed for allowing the subsequent demonstration to go ahead despite it having been permitted the previous year without controversy. There was no prior indication that this year would be different. They were seen as too sympathetic and unable to implement the new draconian programme Bangladesh had planned. The most high-profile casualty was the RRRC chairman Abul Kalam, who was transferred to a role in the textile and jute industry after overseeing two false starts on repatriation. With the help of the media, the new regime portrayed the Rohingya as ungrateful and dangerous to the local community and it wanted to make clear the distinction between host and refugee. NGOs were ordered to employ only Bangladeshi workers, though the government had to relent a little when it realised Bangladeshis did not want to do the camp's harder jobs such as digging wells and clearing sewage canals. Soon after the barbed wire fences began taking shape,

they were complemented with watchtowers for the security
forces. The government also borrowed an increasingly popular
tactic already employed in prior months by Sudan, Ethiopia and
Myanmar. They blacked out the internet. Bangladesh had tried
to limit communication before by banning sales of SIM cards to
refugees, but that had been easily bypassed through the black
market. Now it simply switched off all data signals in the camp,
with the combined effect of cutting off communication between
activists, within families and among NGO employees trying to
coordinate their work. To test whether their attempts to unsettle
the refugees would work, the government quickly brought back
talk of Bhasan Char, which the minister Abdul Momen said
would definitely be going ahead. "If they are not willing, we will
force them", he told German broadcaster DW.[4]

Mohammed

Mohammed's father keeps a small, laminated photo in his shirt
pocket. On one side his son is dressed neatly for an official portrait, the type to be slapped onto permits and school ID cards,
and on the other he is laid out on the ground, his body bloodied.
Mohammed and a childhood friend had gone missing four days
earlier, snatched while they were playing football in Nayapara.
Their bodies had turned up outside a school in a smaller camp
to the south, where the newspapers were saying they had been
involved in a "gunfight" with local police. The two youths were
taken to hospital, where their deaths were confirmed.

Mohammed is not his actual name but his father fears being
identified. We meet outside Nayapara, where he appears from the
crowd, dressed in a striped shirt and *lungi*, phone in hand and
nervously scanning for our car. He jumps in and the car immediately pulls away. We drive somewhere beyond familiar ears and
stay inside to avoid curious eyes. In any other case, his story

might have seemed easy to identify by the very public details put out by the police and press but, in reality, these stories are all the same and there are many of them. The accusations are similar, the locations where bodies were found all close to each other. Details in media reports on a single incident can vary wildly, having a victim's age fall anywhere within a twenty-year range. The names of their parents, their ancestral villages in Myanmar and the camps they grew up in are all reported, but are often false for these young men executed without facing a court. In Mohammed's case, and in most others' also, the named source was Pradip Kumar Das, the head officer at Teknaf Model Police Station. With almost two decades of service under his belt in the Chittagong region, Kumar Das arrived in Teknaf in 2018, around the time Bangladesh launched a brutal anti-drug campaign seemingly modelled after Filipino President Rodrigo Duterte's war on drug dealers. Duterte's uncompromising and popular warning to drug dealers—"I will kill you"—was now being echoed by other leaders in Asia who were also taking note of how he had followed up on it, killing thousands. The scale was smaller in Bangladesh but still around 200 people were killed, many of them in Teknaf, during a rampage by Bangladeshi forces in mid-2018 involving some Rohingya but also a number of Bangladeshis. The operation only scaled down, though it did not stop, when the country heard the shots that executed Teknaf politician Akramul Haque. Haque phoned his family several times that day—telling them first that he had been summoned to a meeting with a local official but, in the third call, that he was being taken to another location for "urgent work" and that he would no longer be able to speak. When his worried wife Ayesha tried to get back in touch, the phone connected but there was no response from her husband; she could only hear men speaking in the background. When she did hear Haque's voice it was as he begged for his life. Screaming into the phone, hoping the executioners would hear her, she pleaded his innocence and asked them to spare him. A gunshot followed. Then another. She did not realise it at the time, but an application on her phone had recorded all of the calls. A few days later she played them to reporters at the press club in Cox's Bazar.

Haque's killing forced the operations to slow in most of the country, but not under Kumar Das's watch in Teknaf despite it being the epicentre of the controversy. Fewer Bangladeshis were caught up in the operations, but the less-scrutinised killings of alleged Rohingya drug traffickers continued unabated. In fact, they increased. Around twenty were reported killed between the execution of Nurul Alam in February and Mohammed's execution in September. The stories relayed to the media by Kumar Das, and occasionally a subordinate, told of police sweeps spooking fugitive Yaba peddlers into firing on them, of bandits hiding firearms in the forest or of child trafficking ring busts. At least two women were killed and almost all of the deaths involved refugees from Nayapara. Machetes, firearms and thousands of recovered Yaba pills were always produced as evidence of the threat the policemen faced. The intimidation was not limited to only a few under suspicion. The uniforms arrived each night and stormed Nayapara's alleys with fury. Batons and bamboo sticks whistled through the air and crashed against the backs of all they came across, whether young men or the elderly walking home from the mosque after the night's final prayer. Dozens were carted off each night, loosely accused of suspicion in Yaba trading or robbery, but were able to buy their freedom by paying bail. It was confusing, at first, for the refugees. They were powerless to stop the police in any case, but were also angry at the real violence they saw from sections of their own community. There were also bodies turning up in the forest, unclaimed by police operations, and continuing intimidation from the bandits. A week after Nurul Alam's comrades exacted their revenge on the paramedic Mohamed Hamid, Abdul Matlab was shot dead—a bespectacled, kind-faced man in his 60s beloved for his education and leadership work.

* * *

Mohammed was picked up at 8 pm on 31 August, at a mosque in the Nayapara registered camp where he'd been playing football. Taken with him were a friend, who was the same age as him, and a younger boy, aged just 17. The details are recorded in a photocopied document Mohammed's father keeps in his shirt pocket, neatly folded into quarters alongside that doubled-sided portrait of Mohammed in life and death. The handwritten letter was translated into rough English with the help of a young neighbour and addressed to UNHCR. Drafted with the other grieving father, they said they "beg to draw your kind attention to the serious facts of injustice killed the two persons ... by the government of Bangladesh." The uncertainty they had been plunged into since the arrests was ended when the youngest boy was released, apparently too young for the fate about to reach the older boys, and relayed to them enough details to reconstruct the chronology of the disappearances. The boys had been picked up in a raid on the camp by uniformed security forces and taken to Teknaf Model Police Station, the same one presided over by Pradip Kumar Das, who had recently been awarded Bangladesh's top police honour for a slew of cases that ended in the death of alleged but uncharged militants or criminals. The boy said they were accused of being Yaba smugglers. "Then," the letter says, "Bangladesh RAB, army, BDR [Border Guards], DB [Detective Branch] and police departments kept them under torture and persecution at a secret place ... our sons were unjustly and unlawfully oppressed, beaten, tortured and broken." The younger boy was first sent to Cox's Bazar jail before his release, but Mohammed and the other man were killed. Their bodies were found at midnight, four days after their disappearance, at a village near Nayapara, riddled with bullets and marked by their torture.

Mohammed's father cannot even fathom the accusations against his son. Though some Rohingya in the camps might be desperate for such income, his family are not. He has another son in Australia who consistently sends money back, enough that their family can get by relatively comfortably and that Mohammed never had to do much more than play football to pass his days. It meant he was not motivated to educate himself or search for work, but also kept him out of trouble. Any memory of Mohammed wracks his father, who seems as broken as his son's body after the torture. The pain strikes him as if physical, forcing him every now and again to clutch weakly at his own heart where that tragic photo sits in his pocket. He believes camp authorities, in collaboration with darker elements, were responsible for his son's murder. In the letter to UNHCR, which was never answered, he said he recognised the need to prosecute the criminals; in fact, he wanted it to happen. But there is a flaw in the system when a camp official collaborating with lawbreakers can blame any young man, who is then killed without a chance to answer.

"Our sons were killed without crimes", the letter states. "We want legal investigations and good justice against offenders and accused [criminals] but our sons are real innocents in the camp. The criminal defendants and refugee brokers of government of Bangladesh, they conspired and gave the fabricated conspiracy reports/complaints to Bangladesh government, killed and shot them, [for] uninvestigated and unproven [claims]."

Mohammed's story did not matter once his body had been dumped and found by local villagers—it was the Bangladeshi police who controlled the narrative. The young men's deaths followed the killing of Omar Faruk, a local who headed the

Awami League's youth wing in Teknaf. He was considered a thug by the Rohingya, but commanded loyalty among locals owing to his political position. Faruk's death was tagged onto the list of accusations levelled against Mohammed, though the deaths of two Rohingya shot down a few days later were also attributed in the media to the Bangladeshi police chasing down perpetrators of the shooting. It all confirmed to the locals the accusations made around the recently failed repatriation that the Rohingya were a mortal threat to them, that their Yaba traders terrorised Teknaf and were brazen enough to touch a local political figure. In Nhila, the closest town to Nayapara, local vigilantes hauled Rohingya from buses and stole their phones, dressing it up as their way of enforcing the government's ban on the Rohingya accessing the internet and travelling. A couple of nights later another mob from Teknaf, loyal to Omar Faruk, rampaged through the Nayapara market, trashing the shops and beating anyone who was in the street. The security forces did not intervene.

Nobi

A text arrived from Nobi—he needed to talk urgently, to as many journalists as possible. "Brother, a serious violation should be reported." It had happened the evening before, during the now regular patrols of security forces inside Nayapara. A group of soldiers entered a Rohingya home while no men were present, just a few children and women. They raped a 12-year-old girl. She screamed to her neighbours for help, but no one came because they themselves feared the men in uniforms. Neither the police nor courts deal with sexual violence effectively in usual times, but this time it involved the army. The soldiers walked away, unconcerned about retribution. The girl's brother later came to Nobi, begging him to take action. They had suffered many indignities but the rape of a child while neighbours were forced to stay silent was an abuse too far, one they had specifically hoped they would be safe from since leaving Myanmar. Nayapara's leaders knew they had to turn to the media, otherwise the soldiers' abuse would be buried. Commanders tried to deny the claim at first and to silence the family—but when they refused to withdraw their claims, and had a case registered after the girl was inspected in hospital, the army was embarrassed into announcing an investigation and promised to deliver justice. But they were furious with the family and camp leaders. They put out extra patrols in Nayapara and stationed some directly outside the girl's home. It did not feel to the family like these extra uniforms were there to offer protection. The girl's brother was warned off speaking to anyone else. Uniforms of all types visited with their old warning: this is Bangladesh, not Myanmar, this is not your home, so do not complain too much.

Unexpectedly, Nobi and a few senior figures in Nayapara received a message from the army, calling them to a meeting at the barracks not far to the south of Nayapara. A while had passed since the rape, which was no longer in the media, so they had no idea that it was the reason for the meeting until they stood in front of an irate army officer. They were immediately berated for taking the rape reports to the media instead of reporting it to the army itself. Nobi was ordered to lie face down, his face pressed into the hot, dusty floor. He was instructed not to move, his sight focused on the floor in front of him, for hours, as soldiers he could not see lashed his body with lengths of plastic piping until long purple bruises marked his limbs. A couple of days later, I met up with Nobi for the first time in months. We had been planning it for a week but he was so shaken by the beating he initially called off our meeting, concerned the army would be watching him. It was the same day that I had been speaking to Mohammed's father and I was ready to head back to Cox's Bazar when Nobi rang me, asking if I was still nearby. When he joined us, he looked tired, his face lined with worry, the marks of the beating still on him. He stepped into our car and immediately asked for us to drive somewhere else, the second time we had to escape familiar faces in Nayapara that day. So, we went to a town nearby and into a little snack shop. We bought sweets and sat down. Nobi was exhausted. The beating had shaken him, his darkened eyes betraying the lack of sleep over the past few nights. In hushed tones, he explained how depressed he had been, how he no longer even wanted to leave his house. UNHCR knew about the beating, but had only said that he should make sure he did not leave the camp. None of it felt fair to him. That was not protection. The bandits he had warned about were still running wild, terrorising local Rohingya while working with Bangladeshi gangsters, and the only response from the security forces had been to attack innocent refugees. In their minds, all refugees were guilty. Maybe that is how soldiers justified raping a young girl, how police so comfortably carted off innocent young men every night. The past year had been a burden and he needed to unload it all, but suddenly fell silent. His face froze and eyes grew in familiar fear because a couple of uniformed police had walked in. It was the same reaction I had seen when we first met in 2015, when he snapped still at the sight of the coastguard by the River Naf. The police officers ordered a couple of cups of tea and took a table next to us, uninterested in our presence. We sat in silence for a few moments, then left.

For as long as I had known him, the way Nobi looked at life had fluctuated. He was usually absorbed by work, driven by the hope that he could invest in his community's future—mostly through his school or helping NGOs. Recently, he had thrown himself into running a Rohingya football team that earlier in the year had won the local tournament, sending the camps into rapturous celebration each time they knocked out a Bangladeshi team. The spectating children threw clumps of dust into the air in spontaneous celebration and danced all the way home. But he was now at one of his lowest points, when current bruises reminded him of old ones, from arrests and beatings, and the bouts of doubt he put aside each time they healed. Nobi's internal turmoil was shared by other Rohingya like him, at war with a suffocating sense of futility each time they launched themselves into a new campaign, but Nobi put himself out there so frequently that he rarely could heal. They had asked only for a few things—for education, safety and justice—but in the past year he had watched friends killed by other Rohingya and the rape of his neighbour. The young people of Nayapara knew the right thing to say was that they were thankful to Bangladesh for hosting them, but it was hard to forever live in gratitude for being allowed to stay in the place where you were born and even harder when you were not allowed to leave it. Many of them hated the people around them, they hated the international community that offered them scraps to survive but did nothing to give them a home.

Our meeting in that town near Nayapara was downbeat but, as our phones came to life after reconnecting to the internet signal, a surprising and slightly strange piece of news filtered through. Argentina, a country the football-mad Rohingya knew mostly because of Lionel Messi, had launched a case against Aung San Suu Kyi. No one knew how much impact that case could have, but it was a glimmer of hope that someone cared. Even more surprising was that a few days earlier, the Gambia had announced it was taking Myanmar to the UN's top court, the International Court of Justice (ICJ), for genocide. Aside from the International Criminal Court, which could imprison the perpetrators of the violence but was still deliberating on opening a case, there was no bigger stage for getting the Rohingya justice. Most Rohingya had never even heard of the small West African

enclave formed on the banks of the River Gambia, entirely surrounded by Senegal apart from where it meets the Atlantic
Ocean. The Gambia had no link to the Rohingya and was no
powerhouse of Muslim politics, but had stepped in where others
had offered words but no action. It had spent two decades under
the corrupt and brutal dictator Yahya Jammeh, but a new government in place since 2016 promised reform, spearheaded by
Justice Minister Abubacarr Tambadou. He had been a prosecutor
in the Rwandan genocide trials in the 1990s and as justice minister had helped women raped by Jammeh and chased down his
death squads. Tambadou visited Bangladesh in 2018 when the
Gambian foreign minister withdrew from an Organisation of
Islamic Cooperation (OIC) meeting. It was an unplanned visit,
but when he visited the camps and spoke to the Rohingya he was
overwhelmed by the similarities with Rwanda—both the killing
and the way the Rohingya had been dehumanised before it. He
said he could smell "the stench of genocide from across the border". Unlike the other foreign dignitaries before him and after,
Tambadou left the camps and the victims he had asked to relive
their trauma with a resolve to act. He had to push the OIC and
his own country onto the right path, one that the Rohingya
would not be aware of for a long time, but when the news came,
it was a rare moment of hope. It was also enough for Nobi to
again shake off a little doubt.

12

JUSTICE

December 2019

Weighty and metronomic, the singular chant "Gambia, Gambia" carried on air heavy with morning dew, a simple dedication to the country that had delivered the Rohingya hope. They were back on their hills near Kutupalong, the camps sitting behind them as their message of support and gratitude was filmed under the dim dawn light, early enough that no one would be ready to stop their crowd of hundreds from assembling. The series of punishments Bangladesh had imposed since 25 August made clear such demonstrations of Rohingya organising power were considered subversive, regardless of how little they challenged Bangladesh itself, but the refugees were eager to say something on this day when they felt that the world might recognise their suffering. The hearings at the ICJ were only preliminary, but finally all the crimes the Rohingya had suffered for so many years were going to be set out in front of the world on a platform that would be reported in all media, and Myanmar would have to answer. Very few Rohingya could travel themselves, so their filmed endorsement for the Gambia's leadership was the one way the refugees had of connecting to what was about to happen, their case fought out by lawyers from the United States, at a court in Europe, while they would not even be able to watch for themselves because of Bangladesh's internet blackout in the camps.

In The Hague, at the grand old building christened the Peace Palace 100 years earlier, all eyes were on Aung San Suu Kyi. Since the 1990s and her Nobel Peace Prize, she had been considered an icon for freedom and democracy, bestowed with awards and honorary degrees almost every year until as late as May 2017, when the City of London Corporation awarded her the freedom of the city for the British capital's financial enclave. But her assent to government in 2016 as State Counsellor, a position created for her because she was constitutionally barred from taking the presidency, confronted her with the challenge of dealing with Myanmar's minorities, who her support base did not necessarily envision as part of their democratic change. Aung San Suu Kyi had negotiated a way into an establishment still dominated by the military and felt no urgency to speak on the Rohingya's troubles, even when pushed. The longer she took this position, the further her status as a peace symbol was eroded until it began to fully crumble as violence ratcheted up and she hunkered down, her words in response becoming increasingly callous, defensive of the military and endorsing of the racist tropes used to dehumanise the Rohingya. In 2012, she suggested the Rohingya should not be considered citizens. In 2016, she was angered that a Muslim—senior reporter Mishal Husain—was sent by the BBC to interview her. In April 2017, she said: "I don't think there is ethnic cleansing going on. I think ethnic cleansing is too strong an expression to use for what is happening." She repeated the army's claims that Muslims were also killing each other. She never used the name Rohingya and asked the US to avoid the term as well, while her allies openly called them Bengali. For the most part, she was only criticised for her silence on the

Tatmadaw's abuse of the Rohingya, which jarred with the world's expectations of her but was initially put down to caution, even when her statements against the minority became more forthright. But the 25 August massacres and their undeniable, very visible horrors put Aung San Suu Kyi's reputation beyond repair and she soon began to lose her honours rapidly. Universities revoked degrees and took down tributes. Honours given by Oxford, Dublin, Paris, and even the most recent from the City of London, were withdrawn. She apparently cared little for what the world thought of her.

There was no real reason for Aung San Suu Kyi to be in The Hague, but she had chosen to stand before the world and defend the Tatmadaw in court—to put herself at the forefront of the case, to become its face—opposite the Gambian justice minister who now seemed to represent the type of freedom and justice world media had always associated with her name. Tambadou walked into the court a man who had stuck by his principles by taking on a cause unrelated to him or his country, a genocide from another continent. Aung San Suu Kyi abandoned her own citizens and principles after she found power. The juxtaposition helped, but Aung San Suu Kyi's presence alone was enough to make the hearings one of the biggest stories in international media, forcing a clamour for the limited seats in the court. Rallies were put on across Myanmar in the weeks running up to the court date, Aung San Suu Kyi's face plastered across banners that declared her as "standing for the dignity of the nation". Activists and artists who had suffered under the military came out to back them now. That the hearings were putting the military on trial was not at all apparent from the demonstrations. On the day itself, another massive rally was held in Yangon, where the proceedings were broadcast on a big screen and loosely translated, while a smaller group made it to The Hague. They were outnumbered by the Rohingya, whose small communities of resettled refugees across Europe had congregated outside the hall, holding a small protest to mark the day. Most could not get inside, though space was made for a few Rohingya brought over from Bangladesh by the Gambia, to see in flesh the leader they had once celebrated alongside the rest of Myanmar.

In the grand, carpeted hall, Aung San Suu Kyi took her seat at the end of the bench, her eyes towards the judges at the front while the Gambian team sat to her right on the other side of the podium. They would talk first and occasionally glance at her over their shoulders, gesturing towards Myanmar's top politician. Their task was to convince the court to order precautionary measures against Myanmar before a full hearing on genocide charges, which was still years down the line. That required making a strong enough argument that there was a reasonable fear of genocide taking place, which needed to be halted before there was no evidence left. Aung San Suu Kyi sat through the opening looking bored, irked even, as an all-star legal team referred to the 2012 violence, to Tula Toli and the villages like it, to Inn Din where the mass grave had been exposed. They dealt with the right that the Gambia had to bring the case, the definition of genocide—which they knew would be picked at by the Myanmar team—and they used the UN's fact-finding reports to recall the realities facing the Rohingya who remained, besieged, in Rakhine State. She blinked constantly, as if struggling to contain her disdain, as it was all recalled, and before that, as Tambadou delivered an impassioned, very human appeal to precede the legal one.

"I stand before you to awaken the conscience of the world", said Tambadou. "When I looked in the eyes of those refugees as they recounted their devastating stories, I could see the looks of fear, of despair, of desperation, and of destruction. The looks of victims of a modern-day genocide. And so we asked the question why? Why is the world standing by and allowing such horrors again in our lifetime? Contrary to the views of many out there, it is not only the State of Myanmar which is on trial here! It is our collective humanity that is being put on trial."[1]

Nobi

As these words were being delivered, Nobi was fiddling around on his phone, hoping the video on the ICJ website would finally connect. Very few Rohingya heard any of these words as they were delivered, though they had tried. Many from Nayapara had decamped to Nhila or other villages. In Kutupalong they walked to the edge of the camp, fiddled on their phones by the new barbed wire fence or hiked to the top of the tallest hills, hoping to find a chink in the Bangladeshi blockade. Some hoped to catch a faint signal wandering over from Myanmar, on SIM cards smuggled across since Bangladesh's clampdown. The elderly had planned to huddle around the younger generation, hoping updates would filter down to them from these screens they did not understand themselves. All they found was frustration. The signals were too weak to load data-heavy video streams and the network was overloaded by everyone eager for information. They fiddled around with their phones for hours until it became obvious they would not be able to listen for themselves. Most had to wait until the night for news, delivered by a few who had gone to the TV shacks at nearby villages to watch Bangladeshi news bulletins. Crowds of hundreds of neighbours gathered at the tops of hills and, silhouetted by solar-powered lampposts, recounted the story of the Gambian minister who stood up to Aung San Suu Kyi and the lawyers who demanded the world recognise the Rohingya genocide.

Nobi awoke the next morning to his phone pinging. The gloomy irony of the Rohingya being unable to watch the closest thing to justice they had ever been offered had brought the internet blackout to global attention. Leaders and figures with political weight made their shock known, loudly describing the blackout as the deprival of a human right—a message that reached the government. Bangladesh had not previously indicated any plans to lift the ban but, for whatever reason, it suddenly did for the second day of the trials, which allowed the Rohingya a way to connect with this milestone moment, to listen in, on the day Aung San Suu Kyi spoke. Even with all they had been through in the past years, having witnessed her silence and barely disguised disdain for them, there were remnants of hope. The Rohingya were not so different from the rest of Myanmar's population under military rule: they had seen Aung San Suu Kyi as the champion of the downtrodden, they had supported her, even joined her political party and campaigned for her, believing that she would forge a democracy that could uplift all the people, including its weakest. This was the day when she spoke not just to the court but faced trial in front of the Rohingya, through phone screens. Instead, she placed her hand over those last embers and suffocated any trace of oxygen that might have been feeding hope. Aung San Suu Kyi stood in front of the court and admitted Rohingya had been killed, that they were now living in exile, but she denied it was genocide, that it was even the military's responsibility. If there were massacres, they were to be blamed on the excesses of individual soldiers or units but not the institution itself. The Tatmadaw, she insisted, should be allowed to investigate itself. She claimed the term clearance operations had been twisted and was not an indicator of genocide or ethnic cleansing, just a routine military term. She claimed conditions for the Rohingya remaining in Rakhine State had been improving, pulling up slides of a football match played between Rakhine and Rohingya teams and a group photo that barely betrayed a smile. It was dangerous to even discuss genocide, she suggested: "Feeding the flames of an extreme polarization in the context of

Rakhine, for example, can harm the values of peace and harmony in Myanmar. Aggravating the wounds of conflict can undermine unity in Rakhine. Hate narratives are not simply confined to hate speech—language that contributes to extreme polarization also amounts to hate narratives."

All the hope these hearings had offered, the excitement at the prospect of justice, instantly evaporated. Anger bubbled in the camps, growing with each word of genocide denial uttered by the woman who was supposed to be the country's hope. Enjoying free access to the internet for the first time in months, Nobi posted on Facebook twenty-three times during the day, each post related to the hearings. He shared clips from the previous day's speeches, articles he had missed in recent times and traumatic footage from Myanmar that reminded them all why these trials needed to happen. He started the day with hopeful messages to the world: he was there, waiting in the refugee camp, and he hoped for a positive outcome. Nobi ended it furiously, sickened by the speech he had heard. "The innocent people, who were killed and burnt alive by the ugliest military are not your brothers, children and parents. You are not understanding the reality of genocide, so you are refusing genocide to defend your poorly trained military. A day will come for you when that same military will fuck you over like they fucked you before for twenty years."

When Bangladesh cut off the internet again at the end of the day, there was no longing to watch any more of these hearings that had reopened wounds. It took several weeks more for the ICJ to deliver its ruling, which Aung San Suu Kyi's pleas and crack team of lawyers had been unable to alter. Myanmar was ordered to protect the Rohingya from genocide and report on its progress quarterly, ahead of the actual trial. There were still questions about what all this meant and whether the UN had enough authority to impose any kind of sanctions on Myanmar for failing to abide by the court's order—especially with China so easily blocking anything from the security council. But, at least, the ruling recognised that genocide was a real threat after the world had skirted around this word for so long.

* * *

Sitting on a red plastic chair in his lime green army uniform, Captain Nyi Nyi Zaw confessed that he had abandoned the 345th Light Infantry Brigade. A pale-coloured, wrinkled sheet of tarpaulin hung behind him to mask his location, but the sounds of the jungle chirped and droned in the background. A faceless voice from behind the camera, belonging to an Arakan Army officer, asked Nyi Nyi Zaw about his role in the Tatmadaw's operations against the Rohingya in 2017. "We conducted the clearance operations to investigate whether there were ARSA members in the villages or people tied to ARSA", said Nyi Nyi Zaw. "We arrested three Muslim men on suspicion of affiliation with ARSA during the clearance operations in Zin-Pai-Nyar village in Maungdaw township on 4 September 2017. There were no villagers there. We suspected and arrested only those three Muslim men tied to ARSA." The questioner asked him where the villagers were. "It was assumed they fled the villages in fear of arrest and torture by us." The voice probed more, about what happened to the arrested men. "We reported to the Battalion Commander about the three captured Muslim men. The officer ordered to shoot those three men dead. We shot those three Muslim men dead by the prawn pond, about 100 metres away from the front of Zin-Pai-Nyar village. The corpses were not buried after being killed, they were thrown into the prawn pond."

It was June 2020 and a week earlier the Arakan Army had released a similar video with four other men in uniforms, claiming they had defected. They all had different reasons for joining. One said he had been abducted, the others because they were promised money for schooling, medicine and food for their families. The first to speak, Myo Win Tun, a Shan man who said he had been forced to join the army, admitted to being involved in killing thirty Rohingya in Taung Bazar, Buthidaung, including women and children, and burying them in a mass grave. He said he deserted because of the racial discrimination he faced within the army and was pushed over the edge when denied the right to go on leave. The others, including men from the Karen and Lahu minorities, said they left because of bullying, because they witnessed their commanders raping and torturing, and because they were tired of the Tatmadaw's treatment of minorities. It was hard to know what to make of the videos, which appeared to be the Arakan Army's attempt to bridge a gap between the Rakhine and Rohingya—an act of solidarity in a way. The men were described as deserters but were clearly in Arakan Army custody, and the group had posted videos of prisoners of war before. It was not even clear how many of these videos there were—the Arakan Army were releasing clips in scatterings and had kept some back.

In September, Fortify Rights announced that they believed Myo Win Tun and another defector, Zaw Naing Tun, had been handed over to the International Criminal Court. Somehow, they were now in The Hague. While the nearby ICJ's process was further along, helped by the Gambia, the ICC, which could actually imprison individuals in the Myanmar army and government, had been building a case. It was not focused on genocide, which was a high bar to meet, but on the charge of forced deportation over 2016 and 2017. In the background, young Rohingya activists had helped ICC prosecutors collect information to build a case, but there was almost nothing like what these former soldiers offered. Neither of their full confessions had been published, but they gave names and ranks of their comrades and commanders; they described their orders to "shoot all you see", to "exterminate all *kalar*", using the racist epithet for the

Rohingya. Myo Win Tun, expanding on the killing of thirty Rohingya in Taung Bazar, admitted to rape and how they killed dozens more as they went between villages. Zaw Naing Tun said they "wiped out" twenty villages in Maungdaw. The story was that they had turned up on the Bangladesh border in August, a month after their confessions were filmed, asking for protection. Bangladesh informed the ICC.

Zia

On the edge of a rubber plantation in northern Malaysia, deadly silent but for the chirping of the birds perched on the branches above, Zia looks out on the rows of gravestones—shaped, in the Malaysian style, a little like minarets—then closes his eyes and extends his cupped hands out in front of him, moving his lips in quiet prayer. He has taken a prayer cap from his jacket pocket to cover his head and is seeking mercy for the souls interred beneath this ground, whose identities are unknown but could include other Rohingya he knew from his old, now distant, life in Bangladesh or the torturous journey that had brought him to this spot. Their gravestones bear not names but serial numbers, used to identify the anonymous bodies found in the mass grave at Wang Kelian. Each engraved number corresponds with DNA samples taken from the bodies and catalogued in case their families might one day be able to offer their own DNA samples in hope of a match. The concept was based on hope of the Rohingya being able to somehow access the world's systems for justice and accountability, to be recognised beyond whichever camp or slum they had been forcibly enclosed in. The reality was quite different. By international standards, they barely existed: a nation registered only through refugee documents and surveillance systems Myanmar had created to monitor their population, down to each household, while denying their existence. There was no prospect of travelling to Malaysia in search of a lost child and no effort made to track the paths of those found. Only a very small proportion of those believed dead were ever uncovered, and families had no way of knowing whether their children might be lying in those graves. Some heard from other passengers of bodies thrown into the sea or left among trees, but for most there had only been an open silence—no call ever coming after the months-long journey or an abrupt end to the contact made through traffickers demanding ransoms. In the void, the only options the families could ponder were of death or the small, torturous chance that their child would contact them in a few years.

Suliman

When I left Suliman in that tearoom in Kutupalong in 2015—where I had met all those men whose sons were somewhere on the sea or in the jungles of Thailand, who kept the traffickers' numbers on their person—he had heard no news of his son. Weeks, then months, passed since the family's heated debates over Mohammed Rafique's journey and his subsequent departure, and they had been forced to sit through it in uncomfortable silence. There was not even a call from the traffickers. It would have at least offered some hope. By the time I tried to find him again, it was a difficult task. The camp had been transformed and the unregistered settlement was no longer a strange, conspicuous island of dust between the trees. Everything south of Kutupalong bazar now looked like it. There was no longer any distinction between the registered camp, the forgotten "hunger camps" where Suliman lived and the newer, makeshift settlements that had spawned and then been swallowed by Kutupalong as each grew into each other.

When I first returned to Bangladesh after the new arrivals in 2017, I failed to find it. It took several trips and weeks of accu-

mulated journeys shuttling along Teknaf Road to recognise anything of that corner of the camp. Though it sat on the roadside,
there were now many other settlements like it, hastily con-
structed in the rush for the limited space. newer, inside one of
the rattling three-wheeler taxis I hired by the day from Cox's
Bazar, I watched the roadside for anything faintly familiar from
that first trip to Kutupalong, something that could take me to
the right place. One day, it clicked. Somehow, the arrangement
of a roadside tea shop and the way the alleyway that led from it
into the camp's interior struck me, despite having seemed so
similar to everything else every other time I had passed. I called
the driver to stop and stepped out of the vehicle with Yassin. We
sat down at the stall and scrolled through my phone for a photo
of Suliman from three years earlier. He was quickly recognised
and a child was sent to search for him. The boy returned after a
minute, confirming he was at home, and took us to him. We
passed the tea shop where we had met for the first time. The
owner, who had sat in the background breaking up stones while
I spoke to the worried fathers, was away but his daughter giggled
knowingly when I showed a picture of him. Suliman's dwelling
was only a few steps away. It was a two-room hut—one with a
kitchen where women worked and socialised and another that
served as a living space and bedroom, adorned only with a single
lightbulb hanging from the ceiling. One of those signs that a
refugee had been here for a while, that they had invested in a
solar panel or battery to break the constant darkness inside their
homes, it also made the small, stuffy room even hotter. Suliman
leaned up against the stockpiled firewood that took up a whole
wall, his face as wiry and worried as it had ever been. By this
point, Suliman had chosen to accept his son was dead. He had
been told so by one of Mohammed Rafique's friends once he
himself eventually arrived in Malaysia. The boy had fallen ill on
the boat and was never seen disembarking. No one had seen him

at any of the trafficking camps on the way to Malaysia. The likelihood had already been discussed in his home, in debates over how long to hold onto hope, as tense as their initial arguments over the 18-year-old's departure, but Suliman and his wife had to accept the news. "How could we feel?" said Suliman. "Our world broke—what did it mean? We cried all the time."

They entered their delayed mourning and over time learned to deal with the grief and guilt, as many of their neighbours had. This version of Mohammed Rafique's fate had an ending. They lived with it for more than a year—the pain of grief still jabbing at them, but less frequently—until one day a Bangladeshi man approached Suliman on the street and asked whether his son had gone to Malaysia. He told Suliman that their son was alive—he did not disembark with others because of illness—but Suliman would have to meet the man in Teknaf to find out more. The revelation was torture. After their months of worrying, being able to believe their son was dead had at least offered some closure, but the chance that this had all been wrong, that he was alive somewhere alone, was hard to process. Had they abandoned him too quickly, while he laboured on fishing trawlers and plantations or languished in disease-ridden prisons? To hope again, that they had not sent their son to his death, could harm them more—especially based only on the word of a man who gave no details. Approaching it was dangerous. It could easily have been a case of mistaken identity. How could Mohammed Rafique's own friends get his death wrong? How would this man know anyway? Suliman feared him. He feared the idea of straying away from the camps to meet someone who was probably involved in the trafficking; the type of person who might kidnap a Rohingya, or at least in Suliman see an opportunity to extort money from a man desperate for good news. If his intentions were pure, why would he have not just told Suliman the whole story there and then? Suliman's head swam with questions and left him submerged. He decided it was easier—safer—to believe his son was dead.

He did not know anything of a DNA register in Malaysia. He would not know how to offer his DNA for a match. No one had come looking for it and no one would. If his son had been thrown out at sea, it was unlikely he would be among the 100 bodies buried in Perlis, in that eerily peaceful cemetery that seems so far from the conditions they died in, but there was no way to know. It took Malaysia until 2019 to launch an investigation into the 2015 boat crisis and then it did not release the results, which would not have focused on identifying the victims anyway. Bangladesh also has never looked beyond the fact that it happened, no one other than the "lowest rungs of the ladder" were arrested on basic operations moving the trafficking victims between safe houses and launching points. There was no investigation into what role people in power may have had in running this complex, transnational ring; how hundreds of people were constantly ferried from land to sea without being stopped; or how both Rohingya and Bangladeshis could simply disappear.

* * *

The apparently monolithic "refugee crisis" had, up until the point of Thailand's mass grave discovery, been treated in global discourse as a very European issue. Thousands were dying in the Mediterranean, attempting to escape conflicts or seek opportunity in the European Union aboard rubber dinghies pushing off from the North African coast or Turkey. Europe battled with itself over whether to accept these people, some of the world's most desperate, or to keep refusing them any route to safety in order to maintain the EU fortress by claiming they were importing security threats. Germany's Angela Merkel offered passage to hundreds of thousands, including many fleeing Syria's civil war, while the EU shifted towards ways of policing the sea. They joined hands with semi-formalised militias at different points along the trafficking route and offered them border policing training to legitimise the task of keeping migrants far from Europe. Europe did not want refugees dying on the seas around it but it also did not want to accept them, so it needed them out of sight.

By May 2015, ASEAN was facing the same problem. Many of its members had already had their reputations tarred by the prevalence of human trafficking in the region, but by casting the Rohingya adrift in their thousands they had created for themselves a situation that drew easy comparisons with Europe in the media. ASEAN could no longer ignore its member states pushing boatloads of people out to sea. Their first step was to reverse the pushbacks and begin emergency rescues of the refugees, bringing them to land where they sorted the Rohingya from the Bangladeshis, the latter promptly repatriated. On 29 May they held an emergency meeting that achieved little itself but set off a series of other meetings that continued even after the Rohingya fell again from the public eye. For a year, they continued wrangling for some common statement of intention, a way to escape scrutiny that could, at least, show they had taken the issue of human trafficking seriously. They agreed, eventually, to the wording for an emergency response system, pledging coordination with each other to avoid deaths at sea. It was announced in Bali, a year after the Rohingya had been cut adrift.

For most, the Bali declaration meant the issue was now out of mind, but Thailand's reputation for human trafficking—whether for sex work, factory labour or fishing trawlers—meant it was especially concerned about being seen to act on the crisis. It was in the worst tier of the US government's index on human trafficking, for countries not even making an effort to end trafficking, which Malaysia had recently escaped. Perhaps that was why, unlike Malaysia and Bangladesh, Thailand launched a criminal investigation that could be pointed to as proof of its attempts to tackle the issue. A new division of its criminal court was established for dealing with human trafficking and the investigation was handed to Major General Paween Pongsirin, a police investigator who took on his task with more vigour than anyone had expected of him. From his perspective it was a straightforward job of "following the evidence", of which there was plenty. They started simply, by interrogating low-level traffickers identified by the victims as having run the camps, to get a sense of the money flow. It helped that a deadly feud between traffickers over money led to their families working with police. What they found was ample, barely concealed, evidence in bank records and on phones tracked through the numbers Rohingya activists had been gathering from families. Millions of Thai baht were uncovered when they raided the homes of traffickers, alongside records of who they had paid—including $1 million wired directly into the bank account of the general Manas Kongpaen. They were made by the Koh Lipe kingpin Pajjuban Angchotephan, who had used his island resorts as stopping points for transferring the refugees to the mainland.

Paween's discoveries led to 153 warrants and a trial of eighty-eight people within the year, including Kongpaen. The evidence against them was even more compelling: there were mass graves, photos and the videos they had used to blackmail innocent Rohingya families. As an interpreter for the victims, Hajj Ismail sat through a lot of it, watching the evidence and listening to stories that shocked even him. "Today this group, today another group—rape, rape, rape", he later described to me in his office behind a small workshop he runs in a Bangkok suburb. Kongpaen was sentenced to twenty-seven years in prison. But by December the investigation had been closed and Paween was seeking asylum in Australia, scared that his success had seen him promoted to a role in the deep south where he would be surrounded by the people he had upset. He revealed how as soon as he started making headway the pressure started to hold back: a sign, for him, that there was more to discover. The longest of the sentences, ninety-four years, was handed down to a Rohingya trafficker who oversaw some camps but was far lower on the hierarchy than Kongpaen or Angchotephan. Paween suspected there were far bigger names involved. In his view, there was no way the traffickers would have been able to hold such large groups of people without being exposed for so many years if they had not had serious protection. Some names were too big to fall. It would have been embarrassing for Thailand for any more in the police, military or politics to be implicated, but failing to go further meant that even with the scores arrested the trafficking network was far from dead. It simply went to sleep.

13

NO PEACE

Zia (April 2020)

From the darkness that concealed the raging sea, exhausted young men and women stumbled desperately into view, their soaked clothes ready to fall apart if not for being glued to their bodies. They were visibly weak, bone jutting against skin with little buffer in between. An adrenaline-fuelled few helped haul other survivors into the hands of rescuers on the coast. They hugged the rescuers, who could only repeat their shock at what they saw, at how many were young women—if they were even yet women at all. The phenomenon of boats capsizing in the night had returned to the Bay of Bengal. This was not even the first. In February a boat had gone down carrying 138 people. Around half of them were rescued and sixteen were announced dead that morning. A couple of days later the coastguard conceded they had given up hope of finding anyone else. For more than a year now there had been land transfers and the odd boat leaving Sittwe, but no route had the potential for mass exploitation like the sea trafficking networks. Zia had spent the last five years warning whoever would listen about the violence of this journey and the chance that it could always return if the Rohingya were not given rights. But during this time there had been so few stories cropping up that even Zia was not prepared for the reminder he received that morning.

He had been looking for a quieter life, somewhere he would not constantly be troubled by the stress of being Rohingya in Kuala Lumpur and where he could focus on his family. He had waited for resettlement, pinning his hopes on Canada, but the process was long and expensive and he was not seen as a priority. So, while he waited, he left Kuala Lumpur and moved to a quieter town where there were still other Rohingya nearby but life was cheaper and less intense. He had been working on his book, the story of the journey that brought him to Malaysia, and the morning's news felt close, like he was being haunted again by the stories he was writing and which should have been history. But he had always known this day would come. "Their bodies will be found in the sea, they will be found in the jungles and the mountains", he said on the phone. Zia was talking about all the places he had seen Rohingya bodies himself. I phoned Hajj Ismail as well, and he confirmed there was little new about the people involved in this trafficking. It was the same people who had lain low since 2015, whom the authorities had put little effort into pursuing. "It's the old network that woke up now."

The *dalaals* had activated long ago, at the end of the previous monsoon, as the mood in the camps was at its lowest. The humanitarian presence had ebbed away, the emergency staff replaced with fresher faces tasked with maintaining conditions in the camps while funding dwindled. It often felt like they were missing and the food had got worse, both in quantity and quality. It had become common to find rocks mixed in with the rice rations. The *dalaals* had kept their heads down when a fully stocked humanitarian mission and wary Bangladeshi authorities watched for human trafficking. Now they could promise jobs for men and a far quicker route to marriage for the young women. As 2020 opened, they were arriving in scatterings that made it seem random but were designed by the traffickers. As before, they had shuttled the refugees from the Bangladeshi coast to larger trawlers in the Bay of Bengal—but instead of taking them to camps, some were now being held on a large boat in international waters. It was a strategy the traffickers had trialled as their camps were being closed down in 2015, during the period when Thailand and Malaysia had begun clamping down on land but were happy for the Rohingya to float at sea. Now, at least until they ratcheted up operations to deal with thousands of people once again, it was a useful way of reintroducing the ransom system. Waiting husbands or families in Bangladesh received those same calls demanding payment, but even when sent the traffickers would not release the passengers until enough had paid up to fill a boat. Then finally they would be sent towards Malaysian shores, hoping the authorities would accept them.

* * *

There were 400 people on the boat that returned to the Bangladeshi shore on that April night. A few hundred more were still at sea, trapped on a floating trafficking camp after the Covid-19 pandemic broke out, unravelling the traffickers' plans to dispatch them to various Southeast Asian shorelines. On the same day, Malaysia announced it was turning away more boats because of the global pandemic that had spread since the turn of the year. Though the Covid-19 coronavirus had first been detected in China in December, it had by this point spread far further and touched most parts of the world. It was probably more of a threat to the refugees Malaysia had sent to crowded detention centres while other countries introduced prisoner amnesties, but now the government claimed refugees might introduce an outbreak and so it would reject them outright.

Bangladesh responded by doing the same, turning its eyes away from the seas where it knew very well that boats were going to be stranded with cyclones and the monsoon about to land. The coronavirus was fuelling anti-migrant and xenophobic policies everywhere in its early days, governments eager to blame the most marginalised for its spread. A complacent Singapore had neglected healthcare for its migrant workers, and it was easy to blame them when their communities suffered an outbreak. Italy, one of the first countries beyond China to suffer a major outbreak, closed its ports to NGO ships rescuing migrants in the Mediterranean and even detained an MSF rescue ship.

Despite Kuala Lumpur's significance as a global city and transport hub for Asia, Malaysia initially seemed to be skirting the crisis, even as South Korea, Japan and Hong Kong dealt with scares and Italy became the warning for an unprepared Europe of the virus's potency. By late June, cases in Malaysia peaked at around 8,800 patients—a small number in comparison with Europe and America, where far more people had died let alone been infected. Around half of the cases could be traced back to a days-long gathering in Kuala Lumpur by the missionary group Tablighi Jamaat. Founded in India, its following transcends borders and its members from various countries were used to congregating to pray, share food and sleep together in mosques. Unsurprisingly, those few days in late February of close, unregulated contact were also responsible for the virus spreading to several other countries when their attendees returned home afterwards. But the focus in the Malaysian media, as well as on social media, soon centred on around 2,000 Rohingya attendees. Unlike other countries, Malaysia's refugee policy meant they were hard to track down afterwards, not least because they were so terrified of the authorities they would not go to hospitals for testing. Malaysia initially announced an amnesty and it managed to track down and test some of the attendees, but as the world became increasingly concerned by the virus—as the emergence of Covid-19 was confirmed as a global pandemic and curfews and lockdowns became the norm—the tone changed.

For the past two years, Malaysia had been governed by Mahathir Mohamad, who returned to the premiership aged 92 offering a break from years of Najib Razak and his alleged corruption. With a nod to his reputation as an outspoken supporter of Muslims around the world, Mahathir took a forthright position on the Rohingya, accusing Myanmar of genocide and suggesting the minority should be given their own state. Such was the break from Najib's government that Rohingya in Malaysia began to speculate that he might finally recognise refugees. In February 2020 Mahathir suddenly stepped down, plunging Malaysia into a constitutional crisis. The replacement appointed by Malaysia's king was Muhyiddin Yassin, a former cabinet minister under Najib, who described himself as "Malay first". In a world of populist governments appealing to the insecurities of their majorities, Yassin's tag was not mere posturing; it translated into a nationalist government that fed from and into social media hatred. When they began to turn away the Rohingya boats that Mahathir's government had reluctantly accepted, they faced criticism from human rights groups and governments that angered Malaysian social media sentiment further—especially when they learned Europe had been no more welcoming to its refugees. During the 2015 crisis on the Andaman Sea, Malaysians on Twitter and Facebook had been eager to engage with articles and statements critical of their government's policies on the so-called "boat people", pointing out the hypocrisy of being criticised for pushing the boats back to sea by a Europe that let thousands drown. Most said they welcomed the Rohingya and directed their frustrations at the Bangladeshis abroad, who they accused of hijacking sympathy for the Rohingya and deemed unwelcome—despite Bangladeshis performing much of the menial labour many Malays considered beneath them. But now the reaction was more visceral and directed squarely at the Rohingya. The tamest bemoaned Malaysia's continued shouldering of a burden much heavier than that of its neighbours, who had consistently done nothing for the Rohingya despite being closer to Myanmar. But much more of it became actively hostile, accusing Rohingya of spreading social ills or even adopting the arguments from Rakhine State that accused the Rohingya of poisoning society. These accounts used the same speech, the same slogans and they shared images with key talking points that could easily be forwarded on social media and through messaging apps. In some cases, it spilled into physical abuse. One video showed a Rohingya grasscutter accosted in rural Malaysia, his UNHCR card confiscated by the assailant, who filmed himself questioning whether the Rohingya man was Muslim.

They also knew which Rohingya and Malaysian refugee advocates to attack. The first targeted was the head of a Rohingya group, promoted by the angry social media profiles into some sort of community representative and attributed with attempting an imagined campaign to demand Malaysia make the Rohingya citizens. Zia was also targeted, accused of the same on messages that called him a monkey while others harassed him with messages saying he was not welcome in Malaysia. He had never been shy about his despair for the Rohingya condition in Malaysia and now his media presence had come back to hurt him. "Since five years, I had never felt this unsafe in this country", Zia said. "It's hurting me a lot. It was never this dangerous before. I'm scared." Malaysia had put in place a strict lockdown by this point, suddenly stranding Zia in another city a two-hour journey from his home. He feared for his family, knowing other Rohingya activists had had their addresses posted online, but was worried that trying to get home could end up with him being arrested and hit with a three-month prison sentence or 1,000 ringgit fine ($250).

New threats came in almost daily, from both anonymous trolls and politicians who had made the Rohingya the subject of daily posts on Facebook. It all felt coordinated, like the disinformation campaigns that had swayed elections in recent years. The language often reflected the hatred that poured out through Facebook in Myanmar and sometimes directly referred to it, pondering whether the Burmese were right. The pages numbered dozens and their users were in the tens of thousands. Some of the pages were run by people who worked in the Malaysian security forces.

* * *

Just before midday on 1 May, knuckles rapped the doors of hundreds of homes in the centre of Kuala Lumpur, almost in complete synchrony. The apartments were in a series of housing blocks christened with grandiose names alluding to penthouses and villas. These neglected towers and the areas around them were now known for their non-Malaysian residents, who were the targets of these coordinated raids by Malaysian immigration forces. The premise for the operation was that undocumented migrants were spreading Covid-19 and needed to be taken in, but they were offered no masks as they were hauled from their homes and forced to march in double-file towards open squares and junctions where the forces had set up tents to process the detainees. They were offered no distance when they were sat down on the road, directly under the sun, and made to wait their turn. Some were released, but hundreds were thrown straight into prison transports so crowded they had to stand the entire journey, unmasked faces brushing against each other, no ventilation to cleanse the air of any Covid-19 particles that might have been exhaled. Only the previous day Home Minister Datuk Seri Hamzah Zainudin had railed against the Rohingya, saying the government did not recognise them as refugees and any groups claiming to represent them would be closed down.

The next day there were more raids, in Kuala Lumpur and around, following the same pattern of hauling tower block residents into the streets and making them sit as they waited to be processed. Landlords were told they would be fined for renting to "illegal immigrants", employers were told the same and wet markets were instructed to ban them from shopping. Yemeni and Syrian refugees were caught up as well, detained by eager immigration officers regardless of whether they presented UNHCR cards. It did not take long before the detention centres filled far beyond capacity and, by June, the number of Covid-19 cases in the prisons accounted for 10 per cent of the country's entire prison population. Other countries had freed prisoners to avoid outbreaks, but Malaysia's already infamous detention centres now had cells with up to 200 people. They were denied food; some were beaten. The sick remained in the cell alongside the others, who felt they were being given a death sentence. Prison guards themselves feared going to work and called for help from the same refugee associations the home minister said he wanted to be closed down. Malaysia was only recording around twenty cases per day and seemed to have the virus under control everywhere apart from in the jails, but as it lifted restrictions it made clear the Rohingya and others would not be allowed to re-enter life as normal. Mosques, the government said, would open for Malaysians only. The only form of schooling open to Zia's daughter was in a local mosque's madrassa, which he paid for, but the new directive on foreigners in the mosques meant that when he asked whether the school would be reopening he was told that it would, "but we are so sorry to tell you, your daughter cannot come to the school". Zia replied with three crying-face emojis.

* * *

Bakthiar ("Member Sahab") was dead. The news was shared in muted celebration, across borders, in private messages not repeated out loud. The relief was not expressed within earshot of his loyalists while they could still seek vengeance. Apparently, the Bangladeshi security forces had tired of his antics, which had caused them to beat him twice over demands that he retain his fiefdom over the "hunger refugees". They announced his death on a Friday morning, after those dawn hours when the gunfight always occurred. Pradip Kumar Das told the media his forces had arrested Bakthiar and Taher, a Rohingya associate, and taken them in for interrogation. The two had apparently then been taken along with police to break up an imminent drug deal they had confessed to, but were ambushed by Bakthiar's henchmen along the way. They had supposedly been caught in the resulting crossfire and killed. Police said they retrieved 17,000 Yaba pills and five crude, locally made guns. It was the archetypal crossfire story. Though Bakthiar's reign over the camps had been ended by the army's arrival, he had maintained influence through the Yaba trade, which had a larger than ever pool of young refugees to exploit as cheap mules and enforcers. It should have been bigger news, the end of a tyrant who had stolen aid and bullied the refugees—but it was about to be overshadowed by another shooting far more momentous, though it did not have such a direct link to the Rohingya themselves.

A 90-second exchange was all it took to end the life of retired military officer Major Sinha Rashed Khan. A former member of the prime minister's personal guard and the son of a former government official, Sinha had apparently retired aged only 36 and was spending a month in the area to make a travel documentary. He was stopped on 31 July, at 10.30 pm, at the Shamlapur checkpoint on his way to his resort on Marine Drive. According to the police account he reacted to a search request by brandishing a gun, forcing the police to open fire in self-defence. Three bullets hit him in the chest. They said they had information about bandits moving along the road at the time, prompting the search, and claimed to have retrieved fifty Yaba pills and alcohol. The story did not stick. Though police said they did not realise who he was until later, the doctors who declared him dead noted Sinha was wearing army clothing.

Sinha was not a Rohingya whose death was meaningless to the establishment or the public, and it would not pass without scrutiny. Immediately, there were questions about whether he really had threatened the police at the checkpoint and if he had, what had happened in those 90 seconds that led to it. A small amount of drugs and alcohol might be illegal, but were not the type of thing anyone with "weight" worried much about being caught with. An investigation was quickly opened and within a week Kumar Das was imprisoned. Not even a year had passed since he had been rewarded for his operations in Teknaf, but the deaths of 204 people on his orders had become a source of scrutiny instead of celebration. His excesses had in fact already caused concern, and allegations that he had gathered vast wealth himself—through trafficking the drugs across the border—had made their way to Sinha during his stay in the area. Not long before he was killed, Sinha had gone to Kumar Das with the charges and had been ordered to drop them. The police chief said he would "destroy" Sinha if he did not. All these details flooded out in RAB press releases and a flurry of investigative reports published by major newspapers. Sinha's death had transformed the routine, unnoteworthy killings in the Teknaf peninsula into a public scandal, with Kumar Das the chief villain. The government had to act and did so dramatically. It apparently decided that Kumar Das's reach was so pervasive that none of the area's police force could be trusted any longer, and so transferred 1,500 officers out of the Cox's Bazar area.

Soon Kutupalong's nights became hell, the nocturnal drone of rural Bangladesh disturbed by gunshots, shouting and terrified screams. This was not what anyone had expected when Bakthiar was killed, but his intolerable presence now seemed insignificant with new tyrants to fill the gap. Within weeks of Sinha's murder and the reshuffling of police, a new pattern of violence had emerged in the camps while the security apparatus was still a mess. Kumar Das's campaign of crossfires had rarely touched anyone of influence, including the most powerful Rohingya crime bosses who were key to the Bangladeshis higher in the chain. The former ARSA commander Master Munna had completely fallen out with the group after refusing an order to reel in his brother Gayseri's Yaba trade—which ARSA saw as a threat to their own chances of dominating the lucrative trade or as a moral challenge, depending on who was talking. Instead, he teamed up with his drug-running brother, suddenly forming a rival power strong enough to challenge the shadow authority ARSA had cultivated in the camps. Their power had extended over the entire Kutupalong camp network, with *majhis* reporting to them and camp authorities aware of their influence, but Munna was capable of chipping away at this dominance and did so with promises. Despite his notoriety he did not hide away from the public, presenting himself as a religious man who handed out money and showed up at the mosques he funded. Like Bakthiar before him, he wore his beard and a mask of piety useful to present whenever counselled by mediators concerned by his activities and the brewing conflict with ARSA. His people used loudspeakers to call to young men, offering payment and finding recruits in the old registered camp to which he became associated. It created an artificial rivalry between them and the newer refugees, one that the Bangladeshi media often latched on to as explanation for any clash between Munna's henchmen and ARSA's—usually over minor arguments near the borders of his territory and ARSA's, which the latter's people had decided to meddle in. But there was also a larger tussle at play. Munna and Gayseri needed a foothold to ensure their Yaba business flowed without interference, but ARSA were not willing to turn a blind eye and risk allowing their rivals' power to grow as they were able to buy out more of the young people. They wanted control back, and stories circulated of core fighters coming down to the camps to help the ragtag members on the ground re-establish dominance. It was useful for the government if they did.

The young man from the registered camp who had taken me to Fatima, the woman who had ended up muling drugs for a Bangladeshi shop owner, had forced himself to leave the camps at night, sheltering with friends in a local village. He referenced that meeting when we spoke. "That Yaba is creating all these problems", he said. "The media don't talk about ARSA v Munna, they talk about registered v unregistered, but this is really just Yaba v Yaba. For Al-Yaqeen and for Munna groups, taking someone's life is very easy for them, they don't care." He had seen how each night mobs from each side raided various parts of the camp armed with sticks and long knives, a few of their armed members firing into the air. They beat and kidnapped men they thought were involved, and some women. To the bystanders, there was no way to tell who was who, as they all behaved the same way—and it reminded them of the violence they had so recently fled. There was no way to speak out against them without the risk of repercussions, so whole families left their blocks, packed up their belongings and headed to family in calmer corners of the camps. Scores of them lined up on the camp perimeters hauling their belongings, as if they were back at the transit camps they had first arrived in.

The worst fighting took place in a single week. Most were scared to film what was happening, save for burning shelters in the distance, but the gangs filmed for themselves their chaotic raids, like trophies of their conquest, of seized men stripped to their underwear, bound by their hands and beaten with cables and poles. Most of the assailants were dressed in the usual shirt and *longyi*, but a few wore army-style imitation fatigues and boots. Some were shot, others were beheaded. Around seven people were killed over a few days, including Gayseri himself, until the Bangladeshi police finally reacted by sending in hundreds of officers clad in riot gear to patrol the camp alleyways. Rumours circulated that they had finally arrested Munna but there was never any footage of his detention, nor any announcement from police forces who would have been expected to celebrate such a victory after recent scandals.

Kutupalong was in disarray, the illusion of shelter it had provided in August 2017 completely shattered now. Though there had been cases, the fear of Covid-19 rampaging through the camps had luckily not been realised—but most services were now barely functioning, and new threats to continued existence in Kutupalong seemed to come more frequently and with more ferocity each time. Kutupalong escapees were now turning up in different parts of the world—especially the survivors of the floating trafficking camp, who had spent months adrift since Malaysia refused to accept any more. Around 200 of them had died already. Some of the last few turned up on the Aceh coast, saved as usual by the local fishermen. Their clothes were so putrid they had to be burned and three of them died soon afterwards. Bangladesh had sent another boatload, which had turned back when the journey became impossible, over to Bhasan Char. Bangladesh said they were being isolated for Covid-19 reasons, but it was really about creating a test population to live on the island. Bangladesh gave the residents of their island camp no voice, even as it sent journalists on sponsored trips to provide reports and convince their own population of how impressive Bhasan Char's housing was. Any Bangladeshi would love to live there, they claimed. But they did not ask any Rohingya whether they were similarly enamoured by the experience. Their voices were only allowed to emerge when Bangladesh arranged a male-heavy delegation of *majhis* to visit the island in September. They were guided around the functional barracks-style structures and perfectly smooth roads in autorickshaws, and shown the shrimp and fish ponds they were told could give them a normal life. But when they were taken to see the women living on the island, there was chaos. If they had been instructed to deliver a message of an island idyll, they had not listened. The women struggled with the security guards trying to hold them back, screaming their demand to be allowed to leave the island, to be taken home with the *majhis* on the ferry returning to the mainland. Though Bhasan Char was hours from land, there was still a heavy police presence that patrolled their blocks, confiscated phones, and that several women claimed had raped them. There was no one for them to complain to. The official report from the returning *majhis* was that Bhasan Char was a suitable place for them to move to.

The buses returned to Kutupalong on 4 December. They waited on the perimeter, by the barbed wire fences that had now been completed. Shuffling through the small door-sized gaps in the fence was a queue of Rohingya hunched under rice sacks filled with their belongings. A few had packed their most treasured items into small trunks. This time, the buses were not going to spend the day waiting. They had already been busy through the night transferring hundreds of refugees out of the camps. They were being taken to a transit camp in Ukhiya, but the next destination was Chittagong and its ferry port. On a nearby hill, the old and young watched eagerly as the buses were loaded, some dashing for a final hug or clasping a hand through the windows as the buses rolled away. Bangladesh said the passengers were all volunteers for Bhasan Char, but their wails betrayed another story. As before, there had been lists produced of so-called volunteers, many of whom seemed confused about how they had ended up on them. Some, eventually, agreed but many felt they had no choice. Some said Bangladeshi officials suggested they should not refuse. Civil society was publicly quiet, though most were silently distraught. They were no longer in a position to make any statement in condemnation. UNHCR were never given the chance to carry out the inspections promised since November 2019: the visits were delayed until they were no longer discussed and until Bangladesh gave up entirely on the pretence of international cooperation. The country bet, correctly, that intentional condemnation would not actually come once it actually went ahead with the plan. UNHCR's response was only to say they would require their own inspection before offering any services on Bhasan Char—a problem Bangladesh solved by inviting local NGOs to work on the island instead.

The ferries were leaving by Friday morning, their passengers sat in neat rows, wearing orange life vests. TV reporters were aboard to witness it, to paint it as a celebratory moment. One woman reporter was followed by a group of young girls as she went about her work, the girls staring up at her as she interviewed and presented to camera. When finished, she turned to them and raised her phone, telling them to stare into it. Some of them shy and others beaming, the girls smiled for the selfie. After three years in Kutupalong, she wrote when she posted the photo on Facebook, this was their Cinderella story.

Mohibullah

Mohibullah had been disconcertingly quiet for a long time, missing since the beginning of the pandemic when he and ARSPH would have been among the most obvious Rohingya partners for informing the camp community about the new danger. He had been silenced, by the dual threats of official pressure and rivals within the camps, who envied his sway and were not shy of spreading dangerous rumours. The prominence granted by his international visits to the UN and the US had not granted protection, even when he asked for it from the UN themselves. He told them he was in danger but no solution was offered to move him anywhere safer. Occasionally some Bangladeshi police officers would sit in with him in his office, questioning any strange visitors while benefiting from the chance to watch over his discussions. The visitors he did have in those months could sense the strange atmosphere—the watchful officers and Mohibullah's own restlessness. The anger around the Bhasan Char evacuations again proved fertile ground for rumours. Many accused ARSA of threatening the so-called volunteers on behalf of the government, but there were also claims that Mohibullah had advised Rohingya to accept the move. Angered by ARSA but feeling betrayed by Mohibullah, some Rohingya, including those who had simply fallen out with him beforehand, began sharing an audio clip on WhatsApp purporting to be a recording of the civil society leader telling a Rohingya man that he should accept the move. It was a distorted recording and the voice, supposedly Mohibullah's, said almost nothing other than to acknowledge the questions listed by the person on the phone about whether there would be food supplies on the island. The recording spread to other Rohingya quickly. "Mohibullah sent people to the island", the rumours claimed. There was no way for him to speak back.

He remained silent, his public presence almost gone. The work of others in ARSPH also fell away, their regular responses to every issue from repatriation to education suddenly nonexistent. Their social media accounts became dormant. There were no more large 25 August memorials for him to speak at and there was no comment as the Bangladeshi government closed down Rohingya markets and shut down schools, having claimed only a month before the pandemic that it would be trialling the offer of formal education with some young Rohingya.

Then, suddenly, when he had already endured his long, enforced silence, he was killed. On a Wednesday afternoon after he had prayed at the mosque, he returned to the ARSPH office to sit, as usual, with a group of elderly Rohingya. They were talking about the rise in the price of food when a group of men stormed in. They were wearing masks and carrying guns and shot Mohibullah several times. They did not leave until they were sure they had delivered a fatal bullet to the leader, who had attempted to stand up. It happened in full sight of other residents and was over within three minutes. Mohibullah bled out on the plastic floor mat where he had welcomed his guests over the four years since they arrived in Bangladesh—the same mat on which he had organised his first campaign to document all the names of the people killed by the Tatmadaw in August 2017.

"May your blood fertilise the seed of freedom. May this mat host the heroes of liberation", wrote Mayyu Ali, a young Rohingya poet who had been with Mohibullah during those early days.

The pictures of that bloodied mat; the bullet casings; and of his lifeless body and red, soaked t-shirt spread quickly, just as every momentous moment did, on WhatsApp. Every Rohingya with a functioning phone received news of Mohibullah's assassination, and any sense of rivalry fell away. There was only shock and fear. His former associates frantically messaged their foreign contacts asking to be extracted from the camps before they could become the next victims. Everyone was sure it was ARSA who had killed him.

His funeral, the next day, was the biggest public gathering since the memorials he had hosted. To Kutupalong came Rohingya from the other camps and squeezed themselves into the space between shelters for a funeral prayer of thousands. Then they stood to the side on the Kutupalong road as a police officer, blowing his whistle, cleared space for his body to be taken for burial. It was wrapped in a white shroud and carried on a metal platform by a dozen men, all trying to help hold him up.

Nobi

Nobi woke to the same screaming that had jolted the whole of Nayapara out of its sleep. The shouting grew louder, disturbing the night in a chorus punctuated by sharp, urgent blasts on a whistle alerting all to the emergency they faced. Nobi stepped outside and the hysteria's cause became clear, the grogginess of his disturbed sleep instantly falling away when he saw plumes of smoke rising from a fire on the western side of his block. His elder brother arrived at that same moment, out of breath, to make sure Nobi had received the warning. They knew they had to run. Their first instinct was to start gathering belongings, but when they glanced over again they saw the fire was spreading quicker than expected. So he told his wife to abandon everything, grabbed his children and rushed out of the door. They knew if they could get to the salt fields nearby they would be safe, the fire would not be able to burn there. Everyone was being funnelled into the same narrow alleyways between their shelters, crashing into each other as they rushed out of their homes. Nobi gripped his children close, but his wife was lost in the chaos. He did not immediately realise it, so by the time they got to the salt field he could not leave his children to join the other young men returning to battle the fire. It had long destroyed the area it had started in, taking only a minute to eat through each shelter. Within moments the whole of Nayapara was glowing orange under the menace of flames leaping 3 metres into the sky. As always, the Rohingya had to respond for themselves. Whoever was available reached for the nearest plastic buckets and filled them at the tube wells with every drop they could pump from them. Some tossed their buckets from ground level and others clambered atop any building that was not yet on fire, hoping the vantage point might somehow make their little water more effective. But the fire continued to grow and their efforts felt futile. The fire department was not far away in Teknaf, but it took them two hours to react to the nocturnal call and, when they arrived, they wasted time searching for a water supply that did not exist. They eventually decided to pump water from a nearby pond.

It was strange that the fire brigade was so unprepared, as if they had not had recent practice in battling fires within the camps. There had been one almost every week over the past months, in every camp on the stretch between Kutupalong and Nayapara. Officially, they were put down to gas canisters, which had always been considered a danger because of the overcrowding, but the Rohingya wondered if that was really the case. The registered refugees had used gas canisters for decades and there had never been such regular fires before—and almost always during the night. Some of the fires seemed to start in strange locations as well, in mosques and schools where there should be no one cooking. But they were usually quickly put out, without loss of life or too many structures, and so few questions were asked. Certainly no one was listening to Rohingya musings about whether this was arson, perhaps aimed at forcing them back to Myanmar or to join the boats heading to Bhasan Char.

But these questions had not yet had the time to play on Nobi's mind as he waited nervously in the field, just on the edge of the camp, watching the fire. "People were watching from afar, crying, trembling, screaming that everything in their homes was burning", he said. While everyone around him wailed, he scanned the crowd for his wife and searched for a space open enough that she could find him. The wait was nervous and felt longer than it was—but after her own frantic search, worried that the children had also been separated from Nobi, she arrived trembling with fear. All had conceded defeat by now; they could only sit in the field solemnly until after dawn, when the fire's last embers had finally burnt out. It had destroyed all 550 shelters in Nobi's block. His students and neighbours were now camped alongside Teknaf Road with nothing but the ash-covered clothing they had gone to sleep in. Among them was Shob Mehraj and her daughter Anu. There was something about the situation that was like that early memory of Shob Mehraj's, in the time before she ever encountered the Myanmar military or state, when the cyclone blew away her home and every home around it, and all she could do was wait in the open until it was over. When the sun was up, she hobbled towards her old home, leaning against Anu, to survey the destruction. It looked like a bomb had gone off. Nothing remained but the thin concrete columns jutting from the ground where she had tried to make the house more stable against the wind, and the tin sheets used for doors and roofing that the heat had twisted into piles of metal on the ground. Like the cyclone, the shelter she had carefully upgraded and arranged into a home of neatly stored cookware and memories was gone. On the roadside she waited with Anu for the expected arrival of the UN. But they only arrived officially. They announced in a statement that "humanitarian partners intervened", but Shob Mehraj could not see much of this intervention—just a handful of bamboo poles that were handed out. They looked measly in the hands of the residents surveying the destruction: adults staring blankly at the rubble and children looking lost, unable to comprehend what had happened. No one came to carry the rubble off or to sweep the ashes away. No one came to help the elderly rebuild their shelters. So they grabbed sheets and strung together the most basic tents, barely tall enough to sit up in, like the ones they had built in the bushes when they fled the Tatmadaw.

Though Zia's mother was in Kutupalong, the rest of his family still lived in the shelter he had grown up in. A couple of hours ahead in Malaysia, the news of the fire had come to him as it was still burning, just after dawn. Again, he was stuck hundreds of miles away unable to do anything but pray. So he prayed. He waited until the fire died down and he contacted his family. They were all safe. Then his mind turned to what was in their home, the belongings he knew they could not have taken with them but which he hoped were safe. Somehow, they had survived. His mother had rushed down to Nayapara to see her brothers and found that Zia's school certificates and personal diaries had survived. Nobi was less fortunate. Every document that represented him had gone. Certificates he had received in school, the proof he had earned to work as an interpreter, that he had been trained as a primary healthcare provider, as a teacher. They were just paper, but they embodied the only achievements he was allowed to have. "Without them, nobody can understand that I'm educated", he said.

Three decades of life had gone in thirty years. In a few weeks, a much larger fire would tear through Balukhali. It would kill dozens and displace 10,000, but the tragedy in Nayapara felt like an even clearer embodiment of the failure of the system the Rohingya lived in. The UN had been a part of Nobi's life since his early childhood, a crutch that allowed him to exist but little more. Perhaps they were complicit in his suffering. They had not helped him return home, nor had they helped him move somewhere more permanent. They played a political game that allowed them to operate in Bangladesh, never testing the government's resolve for fear they would have their access removed. The trade-off was a miserable Rohingya existence, one that could stretch through three decades and as many generations with no promise of change, and whatever little they had scratched out for themselves lost in homes that could stand no more than 45 seconds against a fire. Nobi had long tired of the system he had grown up in—but with the fires and the Bhasan Char relocations, the newer refugees had also shed some of the hope they once had in the international community. They openly mocked the UN's messages of "deep concern" about almost every issue, never matched with any kind of action. The hope that had briefly been drawn from the ICJ case against Myanmar was forgotten and now the world offered nothing, turning its back during the Covid-19 pandemic so countries could focus on themselves. The fire in Nayapara was a lesson that the Rohingya had never been offered peace or safety, just quiet: an unstable, unpredictable quiet; a mere absence of violence. They were offered only the chance to survive precariously, whether in Myanmar or Bangladesh or Malaysia. They would have to sit still—without education or work, without travel or trade—hoping not to anger anyone who might be able to revoke their refuge. Then, at the end of the day, that refuge might suddenly burn down anyway.

Nobi's school was just beyond the area destroyed by the fire, miraculously surviving intact. So he went there and made it a shelter, as it had been in the days when it hosted the refugees crossing the Naf in 2017. But his students had lost all their books in their homes. They would have to rebuild everything. So he went to the plot where his shelter had been and swept away the debris. He bought some bamboo poles and tarpaulin and started building afresh, as his parents had when they were first moved to Nayapara.

"We have been destroyed", he told me in a message the next morning, attaching a video of his walk through the camp's remains. "Everything has been destroyed, even the gas [canisters] and the cooking pots. You can see here all of the sheds and rooms have been destroyed. Now people have become homeless and shelterless."

EPILOGUE

Momtaz

Cradling her son in her arms, Momtaz utters a phrase that has not passed her lips for a long time: *Shanti lage* ("I feel peace"). She can finally flip the lament that so readily rolled off her tongue. Just as saying *Oshanti lage* has always meant so much more than saying she is sad, as it is often translated, she is now expressing an emotion far deeper than happiness. The peace derived purely from the son, Mohammed Rofique, who she is feeding underneath a long scarf. For so long she has yearned to be able to nourish a child as she had done in Tula Toli. She has watched from her doorway the other mothers carrying their children, longing to be like them and knowing that she would have been, if her baby had not been stolen from her arms. Her sparse existence suddenly feels a little homelier with the hand-crafted, wooden cradle swinging from the ceiling. He was born from her new marriage, but the husband has not returned since she became pregnant and the boy is registered to Momtaz's shelter alongside only herself and Rozeya. Her whole demeanour has changed. Instead of crouching, leaning up on the inside of her shelter, she sits outside in the sun, on the small strip of space at the front, cooing at her son to tease a smile from him. The audible pain in her voice has faded, replaced by occasional chuckles. She still has with her the family registration list from Myanmar's regular household counting exercises of the Rohingya. She keeps it folded up, easy to access, a connection to the others on the list who are not with her—especially the youngest, who was not much older than the child she now holds. She does not want to forget, that guilt has not gone and she can never feel complete again, but Mohammed Rofique's birth put back into Momtaz something that had been missing.

Rozeya has started school. She leaves after dawn to go to the madrassa for Islamic teaching and then rushes back. Momtaz sends her off to wash up for breakfast, anxious every moment Rozeya is out of her sight, and the girl darts back just long enough to pinch her brother's cheek and play with him. She unilaterally decided to ignore the boy's official name and call him Abu Tayyib, purely because she preferred the name she had conjured for herself. Just as Momtaz had watched other mothers with longing, Rozeya had asked her mother whether she would again have a brother and so she enjoys every moment with him, whether it's spent playing or cleaning him. When she has satisfied her urge to show him affection, she straps on her oversized UNICEF backpack before Momtaz can put her breakfast on a plate, eager to secure her seat in the crowded classroom. Over on the other hill, instead of going to school, her older cousin Nurkolima serves tea and snacks from a small shop Dildar has set up outside her shelter. They now have their own place to live and their own income, no longer cramped in with Tula Toli's other survivors.

The days for Momtaz are long and empty. She can do nothing but fret over her son and wait for Rozeya to return—never happy about the girl being too long out of her eyesight, though she has regained the childish energy that seemed sapped from her when she first arrived in Bangladesh. Now she feels motivated to zip around everywhere, flashing a full-toothed grin when she laughs.

EPILOGUE

There is no prospect of Momtaz working so she relies on donations or selling off a part of her ration to go to the market and add a little more nutrition to their diet. She goes only when Rozeya has returned to school, the little trips out of her home a rare distraction to the worries that torment her when she is alone. Mohammed Rofique is struggling with digestive problems and has constant gas, but there is nothing she can do. Nor can she fix the back of her shelter—which has fallen away after recent rains, destroying the area she had used to privately bathe.

One of the few things she can do is gossip, with her neighbours or with her aunt who comes to keep Momtaz company and help look after the baby. They wonder whether they might go home, but they have heard the rumours that there is nothing there any longer. Momtaz does not want to return anywhere, she would rather live out the rest of her life in Bangladesh than look again on the ground her husband and children bled into. She has also heard that maybe Tula Toli's refugees will be prioritised for resettlement in Australia. Though she has no clue about where in the world it is or anything about it, she thinks maybe it could be somewhere where her children could be educated. Her son is still a long way off, but Rozeya now loves books and wants to learn. Momtaz knows she needs it, especially in a hostile world she has no father or sibling to shield her from, but she cannot afford to send her to a private centre.

"My daughter is brave, she can be a doctor, she can be a teacher. It is up to her."

NOTES

1. TULA TOLI

1. Author's interviews with Tula Toli villagers, December 2017. Also described in Human Rights Watch report: https://www.hrw.org/report/2017/12/19/massacre-river/burmese-army-crimes-against-humanity-tula

2. Momtaz Begum interview, December 2017.

3. UN fact-finding mission September 2018: https://www.ohchr.org/en/press-releases/2018/09/myanmar-un-fact-finding-mission-releases-its-full-account-massive-violations?LangID=E&NewsID=23575

4. Human Rights Watch: https://www.hrw.org/report/2017/12/19/massacre-river/burmese-army-crimes-against-humanity-tula-toli

5. Available at: https://www.fortifyrights.org/our_films/mya-inv-vdo-2018-09-27/

2. THE RIVER NAF

1. Myint-U, Thant, *The River of Lost Footsteps: Histories of Burma*, 2007.

2. Yegar, Moshe, *The Muslims of Burma*, 1972.

3. Dijk, Dr. Wil O., *Seventeenth-Century Burma and the Dutch East India Company, 1634– 1680*

4. Choudhury,Rishad, 'An eventful politics of difference and its afterlife: Chittagong frontier, Bengal' 2015.

5. Yegar, 1972.

6. Article available at: https://www.burmalibrary.org/en/the-guardian-rangoon-vol-vii-no-5-may-1960

3. THE ESCAPE VALVE

1. It later became Yangon, as Burma became Myanmar, before a new capital, Naypyidaw, was built in the jungle.
2. In Nicolaus briefing as well as *The Times*, 31 October 1978.
3. Lindquist, Alan C. (Head of UNHCR Sub-office Cox's Bazar, 1978), 'Report on the 1978–79 Bangladesh Refugee Relief Operation', June 1979. Available at: https://drive.google.com/file/d/1TIf7EaJLK-mS1U vifNIW992E4fSqHVbi/view
4. Ibid.
5. 'Report of the United Nations High Commissioner for Refugees A/34/12'. Available at: https://www.unhcr.org/en-my/excom/unhcrannual/3ae68c370/report-united-nations-high-commissioner-refugees.html
6. Lindquist 1979.
7. Nicolaus, Peter (Senior Repatriation Officer), 'A Brief Account of the History of the Muslim Population in Arakan', 4 August 1995. https://www.burmalibrary.org/sites/burmalibrary.org/files/obl/docs21/Nicolaus-Peter-NM-Brief_account%20_of_the_Muslim_population_in_Arakan-en.pdf
8. 'A Wretched Exodus from Burma', *The Times*, 5 June 1978, p. 17.
9. *The Times*, 3 June 1978. Available at: https://www.thetimes.co.uk/archive/page/1978-06-03/6.html?region=global#start%3D1978-01-01%26end%3D1978–12–01%26terms%3Darakan%26back%3D/tto/archive/find/arakan/w:1978-01-01%7E1978-12-01/1%26prev%3D/tto/archive/frame/goto/arakan/w:1978-01-01%7E1978-12-01/9%26next%3D/tto/archive/frame/goto/arakan/w:1978-01-01%7E1978-12-01/11
10. Speech available at: https://www.burmalibrary.org/docs6/Ne_Win%27s_speech_Oct-1982-Citizenship_Law.pdf
11. Quoted here: https://www.washingtonpost.com/archive/politics/1988/07/24/burmese-leader-ne-win-resigns-in-surprise-move/1b5896ff-3997-4472-8ffd-d49753838d39/

12. Piper, Tessa, 'Myanmar: Muslims from Rakhine State: Exit and Return'. Available at: https://www.refworld.org/docid/3ae6a6bec.html

13. Government press release, 14 December 1992, cited in UN special rapporteur report to the human rights council in: 2007https://www.burmalibrary.org/docs4/Collected_SRM_CHR_reports.pdf?__cf_chl_tk=LFWp_FRjOF2V2zSLEmscae42A0i3v.G.8ATfJ01IX70-1663953798-0-gaNycGzNCJE

14. Lintner, Bertil, *Burma in Revolt: Opium and Insurgency Since 1948*, 1994.

4. THE ARRIVAL

1. 'Ten Years for the Rohingya Refugees: Past, present and future', Médecins Sans Frontières report, April 2002. Available at: https://www.msf.org/ten-years-rohingya-refugeespast-present-and-future-report-summary

2. U Ohn Gyaw (Minister of Foreign Affairs), press release. reproduced here as part of a summary produced in a government newspaper: https://www.burmalibrary.org/sites/burmalibrary.org/files/obl/docs3/BPS92–02.pdf

5. THE LONG HAUL

1. To conceal her identity, Fatima's real name has not been used.

2. To conceal his identity, Rafiq's real name has not been used.

3. Human Rights Watch/Asia, 'Burma: The Rohingya Muslims: Ending a Cycle of Exodus?' September 1996. Available at: https://www.hrw.org/reports/pdfs/b/burma/burma969.pdf

11. CRACKDOWN

1. International Crisis Group, 'An Avoidable War: Politics and Armed Conflict in Myanmar's Rakhine State' Available at: https://www.crisisgroup.org/asia/south-east-asia/myanmar/307-avoidable-war-politics-and-armed-conflict-myanmars-rakhine-state

2. OHCHR, 'Press briefing note on Myanmar'. Available at: https://www.ohchr.org/en/NewsEvents/Pages/DisplayNews.aspx?NewsID=24446&LangID=E

3. "Six Rohingya Workers Killed in Army Helicopter Attack', *The Irrawaddy*, 4 April 2019. Available at: https://www.irrawaddy.com/news/burma/six-rohingya-workers-killed-army-helicopter-attack.html

4. 'Bangladesh may "force" 100,000 Rohingya to resettle on uninhabited island', DW News, 3 September 2019. Available at: https://www.dw.com/en/bangladesh-may-force-100000-rohingya-to-resettle-on-uninhabited-island/a-50256755

12. JUSTICE

1. Statement by Abubacarr Tambadou, the Gambia's justice minister, at the International Court of Justice, 10 December 2019.

INDEX

INDEX

INDEX

INDEX

East India Company
  British, 24
  Dutch, 25
East Pakistan (1955–1971),
  19–20, 22, 27, 34, 37
education, 30, 36, 37, 47, 49
  refugees, 71–4, 75, 90, 111,
    113–16, 125, 164, 214, 222,
    227, 228
  universities, 3, 31, 34, 37, 72,
    79, 91–2
Eid-ul-Adha, 12
8888 Uprising (1988), 49, 101
elections
  1990 Myanmar general elec-
    tion, 52
  2015 Myanmar general elec-
    tion, 172
  2018 Bangladesh general elec-
    tion, 146
electricity, 31
elephants, 56
English language, 63, 72, 73, 104,
  111, 114, 115, 120, 126, 128,
  148
Erdoğan, Recep Tayyip, 84
Ethiopia, 179
European Union (EU), 172,
  202–3, 211

Facebook, 28, 120, 123, 147, 195,
  211, 213, 221
Faruk, Omar, 183–4
'fat, well-fed refugees' line, 40,
  71, 176

Fatima, 77–82, 218
feminism, 116
fishermen, 3, 77, 92, 94, 219
fishing trawlers, 18, 95, 104, 201,
  203
food rations, 40–41, 43, 59–60,
  69–70, 71, 151
football, 160, 183, 186–7
forced labour, 19, 50, 51–2, 61–2,
  139
Fortify Rights, 15, 166, 197
friendship road, 176

Gambia v. Myanmar (2019–),
  187–8, 189–96, 197–8, 228
gangs, ix, 78–83, 85, 160–68,
  180–84, 214–19
Gaur, Bengal Sultanate, 24
Gayseri, 217, 219
genocide, 4, 15, 33, 49, 187–8,
  189–96
'golden Rakhine', 48, 109, 112
Google Translate, 167
Gundum, Bangladesh, 53

Hague, Netherlands, 190–96, 197
Hamida, 141–3
Haque, Akramul, 180–81
Hasina Wazed, Sheikh, 59, 92,
  131, 146, 158
hate speech, 188, 190, 195,
  212–13
Hinduism, 132, 173
HIV (human immunodeficiency
  viruses), 82

INDEX

INDEX

INDEX

INDEX

(177) BD begun to fence in R camps - Sept(?) 2019 (177) The idea both had
＋ watchtowers (179)   that to R were
                                                                "too comfortable"
(178) BD believed camp commerce, field trafficking, md. R "too comfortable"
comfortable etc. → needs them to move to Bhasan Char.
- NGOs can't pay R + inmates in cash.
(178) Govt. ordered NGOs to employ Bd cooks, but relented when none
                                                        wanted to work there

(189) "Gambia. Gambia" → chants → ICJ

(190) Aung San Suu Kyi denies that there was ethnic cleansing in My.

(190) Obaidul Hassan → 'No one told me I was going to be killed by a Muslim.'
                                              ↑ Beta Bipham - claim
＊(191) ASSK at The Hague ＊ - she traveled there to defend My. ＊ fst. chf. of her caste.
＊(193) News for The Hague focused atta. on't Internet blackout at R camp

                          ← Sept 29, 2021
(225) Mr. Habibullah murdered - rumors both   hold re Bhasan Char.
(223) Every R w a functioning phone recvd news of his assassin. ＊
(224) 1000s gathered for his funeral.   ↳ BD police blamed
                                                                    ARSA

(1a) OSHANTI LAGE (X) Meek Nobi in 2015 — in BD since early 90s @ NAYA PARA
(X) stranded in a state of statelessness → age 28
(XI) 2017 - full scar Myanmar opern. v. R̂. : 700k fled to BD.
(X) Camps now the world's largest → more R̂ in BD than in My.
(X) camps now unrecognisable in their size + filled w/ trauma fresher than ev
CY ASIN
(x) The bk. is abt. the Rohingya pursuit of peace beyond My.
(XII) It abt. the initial machine they pass thru, that has failed to protect them.

(7) Life in Tula Toli described — a cowed people → officially known as MINGYI
pop. 4300 (7)
(8) Tatmadaw assault on Tula Toli = Aug. 30, 2017, a day aft. councillors
they were s...
(9) Methodical rape by army — "Zulam" - oppression. MOMTAZ
(12) River Naf — border b/w BD + My. "...as if the whole Rohingya nation had gathered
on riverbank"
(14) Tula Toli followed the KILA DAUNG massacre of Jan 14 2014
(18) Nobi - a man questioning how it c. be a country beside the refugee camp he
was raised in — let alone the home he was born in across the Naf river.
(18) Rohingya hv a spl. fear at the "sight" of a uniformed man — the visible presence
of a state over a stateless people. (19) Burmese + BD soldiers
(20) 1947 - Some R̂ had wanted to join East Pakistan
(20) Wna described R̂ as national brethren: Newin's 1962 Coup did that, whe
cracked down on frontier minorities, incl. the R̂.
(21) 1978 - 200k R̂ forced out by Newin
(21) 1982 Citizenship (L) excluded the R̂ x (A) Newin "(My + BD)"
(21) Rohingya - bounced b/w nations that didn't want them" (My + BD)
(21) Rohingya - bounced b/w nations that... there were no R̂ in Burma before the British (1824)
(23) official My. history says there were no R̂ in Burma before the British.
(23) But the R̂ presence predates the British.
(27) characteristics of R̂ camp — mixtures.

(29) Nobi's lament.

(30) [1978] - Sheb Mehraj — 'no violence yet : they (R̂) had been
forgotten'. (31) They were on the periphery of Burma but they did...
yet feel hated!
(31) Even a R̂ middle-class (34) one form of Rohingya persecution on statelessn...
(39) Opa. Nofamin - Dragon King — b/w March + July 1978, 200k R̂ fled to BD
(40) July 1978: BD signed a repatriation deal w/ Burma — "we are not going back.
to mk. the refugees so comfortable that they want to go back." (X)
(46) 1982 Citizenship (L) voided the documents of all those R̂ who had
meticulously proved they belonged, during opern. Nofamin.
(46-7) Newin on the importance of exclusion x